SHAKESPEARE'S
SONNETS

{ *Freshly Phrased* }

Timeless Verse Retold
for Modern Readers

SHAKESPEARE'S
SONNETS

{ *Freshly Phrased* }

Timeless Verse Retold for Modern Readers

Joseph Gallagher

FALL
RIVER
PRESS

Fall River Press
122 Fifth Avenue
New York, NY 10011

ISBN: 978-1-4351-1034-2

Jacket design by Jim Sarfati

Printed and bound in the United States of America

1 3 5 7 9 10 8 6 4 2

Dedication

Contents

Author's Note   7

Overview   8

Introduction   9
  Abbreviations   19
  Words Curiously Capitalized and Italicized   20

The Sonnets   21
  Introductory Note to Sonnet #1   22
  Sonnets 1–154   24

Appendix   332
  Was There Really a Shakespeare?   332
  How Do You Spell That?   333
  More Sonnet Context   334
  Technicalities   339
  Shakespeare's Sonnets: Curiosities   340
  Words, Words, Words   341
  Sonnet Words   343
  Longest, Shortest Plays and All the Poems   344
  Resources   345

First Line Index   346

Author's Note

Long ago I heard of a man who so loved Shakespeare that he kept one of his masterpieces unread. He wanted to look forward to savoring a fresh marvel on his deathbed.

Through the decades that story has haunted me. As I neared seventy, I realized that I had saved far too much material for my deathbed. So my resolution was to read all of the Bard in one year. It took me fifteen months. I had no illusions that I was fully appreciating the near million words I was reading. That total included biographies and commentaries.

I was struck by how many of the 154 sonnets, brief as they are, proved virgin territory for me, and how difficult many were. I looked for help in the form of paraphrases, but discovered that I couldn't find any book dedicated to plain, loyal rephrasings of all the four-hundred-year-old originals.

So my retirement project became the production of such an aid. It took more than four years off and on. I am grateful to friends who in various ways helped me with this task, especially John Abrahams, Keith Boisvert, John Dietzenbach, Ruth Eger, Russ Forrester, Pete Garthe, Joseph Gossman, Ed Griswold, Tess and Gus Hoffman, Noreen and Bob Lidston, John Maningas, Kathy and Larry Mayer, Judy McGinn, Marita Podder, Mike Schmied, Laura Malick Sontag, Rusty Shaughnessy, Forrest Schoenbachler, Eleanor Sprankle, and Richard Troy.

Keenly mourned major benefactors are Josephine Jacobsen, Bill Mueller, Bob Sprankle, Charlotte and Tom Mancine. Cordial thanks to all, especially to the unwittingly but not ungratefully unnamed. —JOSEPH GALLAGHER

Overview

The 154 sonnets of 1609 A.D. have two unbalanced parts:

PART ONE: Sonnets 1 through 126 (about 80 percent of the total) mostly pertain to *a man right fair*, featuring:

> 1/A) one SPEAKER: William Shakespeare; never self-identified, but occasionally playing with the word *Will*;
>
> 1/B) one specific ADDRESSEE: a young man never named; at first stubbornly unmarried, handsome, and seemingly highborn and wealthy;
>
> 1/C) one unnamed MISTRESS of 1/A, stolen by 1/B (Ss 40–42);
>
> 1/D) several unnamed POETS trying to steal the favor of 1/B from 1/A: Ss 78–80, 82–86.

Themes: survival through progeny and poetry; inner and outer beauty; love and friendship; decay and death; absences; rivalries.

PART TWO: Sonnets 127 through 154 (28 poems, or about 20 percent) mostly pertain to *a woman coloured ill*, featuring:

> 2/A) one SPEAKER: William Shakespeare, never self-identified, but much playing on the word *Will*;
>
> 2/B) one specific ADDRESSEE: the Dark Lady: the Speaker's mistress, probably the woman of 1/C;
>
> 2/C) one male FRIEND, stolen from 2/A by 2/B (S144), probably the Youth of 1/B.

Themes: standards of beauty; lust; betrayal; promiscuity; deceit; mad infatuation; blindness; frustration.

Introduction

Oh I could write a sonnet/about your Easter bonnet.
                                        —IRVING BERLIN

*He is a fool who cannot make one sonnet; he is mad who
makes two.*   —JOHN DONNE
                          (who made several dozen)

As if in a conspiracy of "s"s, in the sixteenth century (the century of Shakespeare's birth) leading English poets like Surrey, Sidney, Spenser, and Sir Thomas Wyatt began imitating the fourteen-line Italian verse-form called the *sonetto* (a sounding, a little song; cf. *sonata*).

Italians such as Dante, Petrarch, and Michelangelo had already composed such "songs." Shakespeare's Spanish contemporary, Lope de Vega, wrote 1,587 of them. Later poets like Milton, Wordsworth, Keats, Elizabeth Browning, the Jesuit Hopkins, Rilke, and Edna St. Vincent Millay would contribute to the persistent tradition.

The aforementioned Dante (1265–1321) is credited with the earliest recorded use of a name for the form: *sonetto*. That word appeared in his *La Vita Nuova* (c. 1293).

The earliest printed record of the English word *sonnet* dates from 1557, seven years before Shakespeare's birth.

Though still usually featuring a man singing the praises of an idealized woman, the early English sonnet somewhat modified the rules of the foreign form. (At times a brief love lyric was also called a sonnet, even though it made no effort to follow the rules.)

The medieval knight, to impress and honor his fair lady, fought a joust on a field of chivalry. The gallant sonneteer, however, struggles with the limitations of space, rhythm, and rhyme to win his struggle with the sonnet form, and then present it as a victory gift to his beloved.

As a kind of Houdini in reverse, the sonneteer compresses his thoughts and feelings into a verbal straitjacket. If the fit looks handsome, comfortable, even natural, then both his skill and his devotion have been vindicated.

By the early 1590s, sonnet-writing was all the rage in England, especially in Shakespeare's adopted London. In 1598 a literary critic mentioned the "sugred sonnets," which the witty Shakespeare was circulating among his "private friends."

Publication would reveal that not all of his sonnets were all that sugary, and that at least some might have been meant to be understood only by such friends.

It wasn't until 1609 that a collection of 154 of his sonnets appeared, listed by Arabic numbering. Its title was *Shakespeare's Sonnets*, described as "Never Before Imprinted," though (with slightly different wording) sonnets 138 and 144 had already been made public a decade earlier—without their author's permission.

That 1609 edition is referred to as *Q*, for *quarto*—a book composed of single sheets of paper folded into quarters and thus providing eight sides to each "signature." Of the perhaps 1,000 copies of *Q* printed, only thirteen are known to survive.

One of the longest sonnet sequences ever published, Shakespeare's *Q* has more lines than *Macbeth*, and four more units than the *Book of Psalms*—the Bible's largest book. (The *King James Bible*, incidentally, was published shortly after *Q*.) The dedication in *Q* is unusual and extremely controversial. (See sidebar on page 12.)

The sonnets themselves frequently speak of being a lasting monument to a young man's beauty and virtue, and the lettering of the dedication suggests the carving on a monument.

Obviously not composed by Shakespeare, this 1609 dedication raises famous problems. For his two earlier books of poetry, Shakespeare himself wrote the customary flowery dedications—both of them to a young man named Henry Wriothesley ("H.W."/*rizly* or *rosly*), third Earl of Southampton, and a darling of the court of Queen Elizabeth I.

(The Southampton name endures in a major transatlantic port in extreme south central England. De la

Warr, the first English governor of Virginia, named Hampton Roads after Henry, who was a stock-holding member of the Virginia Company, which founded Jamestown in 1607—two years before the *Sonnets* were published.)

The Notorious 1609 Dedication

ORIGINAL	PARAPHRASE
TO • THE • ONLIE • BEGETTER • OF •	AS • HE • SETS • FORTH •
THESE • INSVING • SONNETS •	ON • THE • WELL-WISHING •
MR. W.H. ALL • HAPPINESSE •	ADVENTURE • OF • PUBLISHING •
THAT • ETERNITIE •	AND • THE • FOLLOWING •
PROMISED •	SONNETS •
BY •	T.T. [Thomas Thorpe]
OVR • EVERLIVING • POET •	WISHES •
WISHETH •	FOR • THEIR • SOLE • BEGETTER •
THE • WELL-WISHING •	MR. W.H.
ADVENTVRER • IN •	AND • HAPPINESS •
SETTING •	ALONG • WITH • THAT ETERNITY •
FORTH •	PROMISED • HIM • BY • OUR •
T.T.	EVERLIVING • POET •

This third dedication, however, was signed by T.T., who calls himself the publisher. Those initials had already appeared on the title page, where it is said that G. Eld printed the sonnets for T.T. We know that T.T. was Thomas Thorpe, noted for procuring unpublished manuscripts, including ones by poets Christopher Marlowe and Ben Jonson. Does the dedication by the publisher mean that this volume was pirated, i.e., published without the author's permission?

As the dedication implies, the *Sonnets* are supposed to bring eternal fame to a specific but unnamed man. If literal, that promise would seem to require that the man be publicly acknowledged in some form, and that at least some of the sonnets about him be published. But there is no indication that Shakespeare ever published any of them elsewhere, nor is there any record of Shakespeare's disapproval of Thorpe's publishing "adventure."

Unlike the sonnet sequences already published and composed by other English poets such as Sidney and Spenser, and unlike Shakespeare's two earlier books of poetry, the 1609 *Quarto* was not a marked success. (Yet today, four hundred years later, the *Sonnets* is his best seller.) For one thing, after a brief revival following the 1603 death of Elizabeth and the accession of James I as her successor, the sonnet vogue had died out in England by the time Thorpe's crucial and historic edition was published. Interestingly, Shakespeare did not publish a sonnet on the Queen's death. The omission was noticed and criticized.

More than a century and a half would elapse before there was a true second edition of the 1609 *Sonnets*. (It has been theorized that the book may even have been suppressed in its author's lifetime.) By contrast, his *Rape of Lucrece* underwent five reprints before his death; his *Venus and Adonis* chalked up ten editions before

1616, and was arguably the best-selling poem of the Elizabethan era.

In the meantime a few imperfect versions appeared, which omitted some of the sonnets, altered their numbering, and, on sexually embarrassing occasions, changed "he" to "she"—the reverse of what happened at first to some of Emily Dickinson's poems concerning a woman friend.

No handwritten originals of the *Q* sonnets survive. For reasons related to customary Shakespearean spellings and abbreviations, scholars argue that the typesetters (probably two) worked from a copy that was not the poet's original. It was not unusual for scribes and typesetters to do their own punctuating of poetry, and follow their own spelling preferences. That first edition exhibits enough flaws to suggest that the proofs were not corrected by the poet, who, however, has been described as "incurably easygoing."

One theory argues that he hurriedly left London to avoid a recurrence of the plague, but not before authorizing his publisher to formulate the dedication. That arrangement also gave the author deniability. (And surely, if the notably modest Bard had composed the dedication, would he have called himself an "immortal poet"? Still, it's true that in some of the sonnets, he ascribes immortality to their words and subject.)

Shakespeare's Sonnets are radical in tone and theme. Though unusually straightforward in some respects, they can be quite difficult for modern readers—thanks to their often compact, allusive, elliptical, and highly metaphoric quality, and thanks to four centuries of vocabulary and stylistic changes.

John Benson (not to be confused with Ben Jonson) published an adulterated "second" edition in 1640. He assured his readers that they would find the sonnets "Seren, cleere, and eligantly plaine;" they would not "perplexe your braine," since they contained "no intricate or cloudy stuffe to puzzell intellect."

One eminent modern critic, though, has insisted: "*Shakespeare's Sonnets* are hard to think about. They are hard to think about individually, and they are hard to think about collectively." (Stephen Booth, *An Essay on Shakespeare*, 1969.) The same expert has remarked of them: "We know what they mean, but we don't know what they say." In brief, they are clear until you peer.

Whence the following paraphrases, which are just one person's interpretations. (May they send the reader more confidently back to the originals, printed herein next to the paraphrases.) In the words of Jonathan Bate, a recent biographer of Shakespeare, "The genius of the sonnets is their power to generate readings" (i.e., interpretations).

The interpretations will be heavily influenced by whether the reader (or the critic) believes that the *Sonnets* are a) essentially autobiographical and factual; or b) essentially fictional—i.e., just literary exercises on various romantic themes; or c) based on real life experiences, but developed beyond the facts in various imaginative ways. In my notes, I am assuming that Shakespeare had a deeply affectionate but stormy bond with the *fair young man* in the *Sonnets*.

One radical feature of the *Sonnets* is this strikingly affectionate male-to-male aspect of so many of them— though Shakespeare was not the first English sonneteer to deal with friendship between men. The Earl of Surrey pioneered this theme in English sonnetry before his execution at age thirty in 1537.

Whether the male friendship theme is fact or fiction in the *Sonnets*, the ardor of the relationship has soured the "sugred" sonnets for some readers. When the poet William Wordsworth famously claimed that in the *Sonnets* Shakespeare "unlocked his heart," another poet, Robert Browning, famously huffed, "If so, the less Shakespeare he!"

In any case, the three dozen Shakespeare plays reveal a genius of "infinite variety," a man who had an astonishing understanding of every human feeling and possibility.

The homoerotic flavor of some sonnets goes unnoticed by many a reader because most of them talk to an unidentified "you" or "thou." The "sexuality" of the *Sonnets* is further complicated by three other facts:

1) in Shakespeare's day, unquestionably heterosexual men spoke to one another in quite loving terms—though they did not normally obsess about another man's physical beauty and call him "lover";

2) in the tradition of patron-client relationships, a poet was expected to use extravagant terms of flattery;

3) in real life, Shakespeare had a wife and begot three children. (As he says in Sonnet 121: "I may be straight.") In the *Sonnets* he tells of having had at least one mistress—whom he unwillingly shared with his special male friend.

But back to the "onlie begetter" and the presumed chief addressee of the *Sonnets*. There is no doubt that he was an actual person. But who is this "Mr. W.H"? If the initials are correct (and not deliberately reversed), he may be William Herbert (1580–1630), the prestigious third Earl of Pembroke, a notable patron of writers.

He was sixteen years younger than Shakespeare, and could have been in his mid-teens when the thirtyish poet was presumably writing the "please-reproduce-yourself" sonnets. In the England of those days, marriage was legally possible at fourteen, and we know that Herbert resisted marriage.

It was to this Herbert that the famous 1623 *First Folio* of Shakespeare's plays (which did not include the *Sonnets*) was dedicated. The two editors of that invaluable *Folio*—a copy sold for $6.2 million recently—were Henry Condell and John Heminges. These were both friends and fellow-actors of the Bard, who left each of them a gift in his celebrated last will.

In their dedication of this *First Folio* these knowledgeable friends speak of the great generosity that

William Herbert (and his brother Philip) showed to the living Shakespeare. As they put it, the brothers "have pursued both them [the plays], and their Author when living, with so much favor."

If Herbert was "W.H.," publisher Thorpe may have used only his initials fourteen years earlier, in 1609, out of concern that some of the sonnets might prove embarrassing. (After all, dedications were supposed to please the honoree into making a monetary gift.) Or the initials might have been reversed as a disguise—"W.H." for "H.W." The dedicatee could then have been Henry Wriothesley, third Earl of Southampton (1573–1624), a distant cousin of the Bard. It was to him (as mentioned earlier) that Shakespeare had already openly dedicated his first two books of poetry: *Venus and Adonis* (1593—about a man who resists a woman), and *The Rape of Lucrece* (1594—about a woman who resists a man). "H.W." could have been in his early twenties when the poet was urging him to marry.

Since, however, some nameless "Dark Lady" triggered the final 28 sonnets, it is hard to see how "Mr. W.H." (or "Mr. H.W.") could be, as the dedication claims, the "onlie begetter" of the volume—unless the beggeter is the person who handed the *Sonnets* over to the printer. If that's the case, though, what is the meaning of the "eternitie promised him by our ever-living poet"?

One ingenious theory suggests that "W.H." is an easy misprint for "W.S.," the poet himself, to whom T.T.

wishes to ingratiate himself as "well-wishing." Though it seems a stretch, the "ever-living" (i.e., dead) poet could then be Edmund Spenser (?1552–1599), who had actually died a decade earlier, and who had written of the immortality to be gained by the author of sonnets (such as the *Amoretti*, which he himself had composed).

Among various extreme theories, one sees the "ever-living poet" as God Himself; another sees the *Sonnets* as written to Queen Elizabeth (who successfully resisted marriage), or even written by her, if not by Christopher Marlowe, who (went one theory) wasn't truly murdered, but went into hiding for the rest of his days!

Understandably, then, this problematic thirty-word dedication has been called "the Sphinx" of Shakespeare studies. More will be said on this subject and others in the notes appended to the sonnet paraphrases that follow. An appendix will offer additional pertinent data.

ABBREVIATIONS IN THE NOTES

W.S. = William Shakespeare, the voice of the *Sonnets*
S = sonnet
Ss = sonnets
L = a line within a sonnet / Ls = lines
H.W. = Henry Wriothesley (1573–1624), the third Earl of Southampton, the possible "begetter" of the 1609 *Quarto* (*Q*) of the *Sonnets* (with his initials reversed)

W.H. = William Herbert (1580–1630), the third Earl of Pembroke, another possible "beggeter" of the *Sonnets*

Words Curiously Capitalized and Italicized

In the *Sonnets*, *Rose* is mentioned and capitalized thirteen times: in Ss 1, 35, 54, 67, 95, 98, 99, 109, and 130. It is italicized only in S1, but never begins with a small letter—unlike all other *Sonnet* flowers.

Will (the poet's name) receives this special treatment in three sonnets: 135, 136, and 143. Similarly treated in one sonnet only are: *Audit* (S4), *Hews* (Hues) S20, *Adonis, Helen's, Grecian* (S53), *Statues, Mars* (S55), *Intrim* (Interim) S56, *Alien* (S78), *Eaves* (Eve's) S93, *Saturn* (S98), *Satire* (S100), *Philomel* (S102), *Autumn* (S104), *Abisme* (Abyss) S112, *Alcumie* (Alchemy) S114, *Syren* (Siren) S119, *Audite* (Audit), and *Quietus* (Discharge) S126.

There seems to be no scholarly agreement on the significance, if any, of the unusual printing style of most of these words.

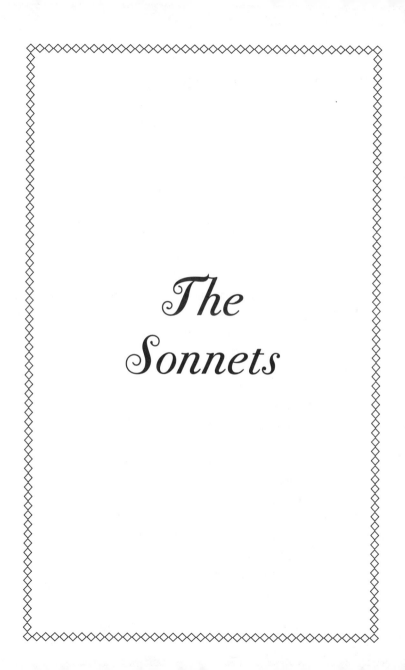

The
Sonnets

Introductory Note to Sonnet #1

Along with sixteen of the first seventeen *Sonnets*, the opening one directly urges a very handsome youth to produce an heir. A widely accepted period for the composition of most of the *Sonnets* is the 1590s.

During the decade or so before they were published, the author may have made revisions, and added sonnets dating from the 1600s. *We have no proof, however, that the 154 sonnets were printed in the order of their composition, nor even that the order was chosen by the poet himself.*

In the original 1609 printing of this introductory sonnet, the word *Rose* in line 2 is mysteriously capitalized and italicized. There is evidence that the Earl of Southampton's family name "Wriothesley," contained a "rose" sound.

Is *Rose* then one clue that this Earl is the youth who inspired most of the *Sonnets*, though he was only nine years younger than the poet? If "W.H." was indeed the Earl of Southampton, he finally underwent a kind of shotgun marriage when he was twenty-five, producing an heir in 1605.

When the Earl was about fifty, he led an expedition against the Spanish in the Netherlands. There, both he and his nineteen-year-old heir died of a fever—the son actually five days before the father. The year was 1623. Shakespeare was seven years dead, but the historic *First Folio* had just been published—though without the *Sonnets*.

Along with three daughters, Southampton had a second son. He became the fourth Earl, but died without issue. As the poet feared, time and death vanquished the fair youth and his personal male line.

What of the other candidate for being "W.H."—William Herbert, third Earl of Pembroke? He had two children—both boys: one illegitimate (1601) and one legitimate (1620). Both died shortly after birth. So he left behind no heirs at all.

Sadly, the poet himself would lose his only male heir, the twin Hamnet, who lived to be only eleven years old. The direct family line died out in 1670. By one counting, made in the mid-1900s, more than 400 descendants of Shakespeare's sister Joan (and her husband William Hart) were said to be still living, some in Salt Lake City.

The sole original version of Shakespeare's *Sonnet 1* uses spellings and punctuation rules which have changed over the past four centuries. In addition to typos, misreadings of the original manuscript (now lost) are common.

For example, besides all the "s"s that look like "f"s, you find *beauties* for beauty's, *neuer* for never, *owne* for own, *fewell* for fuel, *cruell* for cruel, *wast* for waste, *pitty* for pity, *eate* for eat, *worlds* for world's, and *graue* for grave.

Editors who try to modernize the text have differing standards for so doing. So, there is no authoritative, definitive version of *Shakespeare's Sonnets* other than the defective and difficult 1609 original. The version used in this book is a composite taken from a number of the many versions available.

1

From fairest creatures we desire increase,
That thereby beauty's **Rose** *might never die,*
But as the riper should by time decease,
His tender heir might bear his memory:
But thou, contracted to thine own bright eyes,
Feed'st thy light's flame with self-substantial fuel,
Making a famine where abundance lies,
Thyself thy foe, to thy sweet self too cruel.
Thou that art now the world's fresh ornament
And only herald to the gaudy spring,
Within thine own bud buriest thy content
And, tender churl, mak'st waste in niggarding.
  Pity the world, or else this glutton be,
  To eat the world's due, by the grave and thee.

REPRODUCE, NARCISSISTIC YOUTH!

EVERYBODY WANTS the loveliest human beings to reproduce themselves and thereby protect the *Rose* of their beauty from total annihilation. Thus, when a handsome father eventually dies, his youthful heir will preserve the memory of his grace.

But, instead of spreading your light, you have diminished it by wedding it to your own shining eyes. By expending all your fuel on yourself, you have turned abundance into a famine. You are thus your own enemy, and too cruel to your own sweet self.

In your youth you are now the world's fresh ornament, the total herald of a joyful springtide. But you are burying your potential within your own petals, and, sweet rascal, you are being wasteful by your stinginess.

Have pity on the world—or else be a glutton who allows himself and the grave to consume what is the world's due.

Note: Narcissus drowned while admiring his own watery image. / In the original printing, each sonnet begins with an enlarged letter (two lines deep), followed, oddly, by a one-line capital letter. / L2: only here, out of 13 occurrences, is *Rose* both capitalized and italicized. It never starts with a small letter. / L8: *sweet self* appears in the first and the last (S126) of the Fair Youth poems, but only twice in between (S4 and S114).

2

When forty winters shall besiege thy brow,
And dig deep trenches in thy beauty's field,
Thy youth's proud livery so gaz'd on now,
Will be a tatter'd weed, of small worth held:
Then being ask'd, where all thy beauty lies,
Where all the treasure of thy lusty days,
To say, within thine own deep-sunken eyes,
Were an all-eating shame and thriftless praise.
How much more praise deserv'd thy beauty's use,
If thou couldst answer, "This fair child of mine
Shall sum my count, and make my old excuse,"
Proving his beauty by succession thine!
    This were to be new made when thou art old,
    And see thy blood warm when thou feel'st it cold.

BEGET A JUSTIFYING CHILD!

WAIT TILL FORTY WINTERS have warred on your face, and plowed deep wrinkles into its beauty! Then your proud uniform of youth—now so much admired—will be worn to tatters and held in slight esteem.

Someone might ask you then what happened to your good looks and to all the gifts of your lusty manhood. It would be an absolute disgrace and hollow praise if you replied that they lingered on in your deep-sunken eyes.

It would be much more laudable if you could point to someone whose beauty would prove that he is yours, and say: "This winsome child of mine must be added to my account, and will justify my old age."

Such a claim will renew you when you are elderly, and show you the former warmth of your blood when you feel it cold.

Note: L1: in the poet's day, 40 was old, the average age of death being about 30. W.S. lived to be 52, and was in the minority who survived to see a grandchild. / L4: *weeds* (as in "widow's weeds"): garments. / L5: *beauty*, a favorite quality of *Shakespeare's Sonnets*, already cited in S1, and thrice mentioned here. We will meet it some 70 more times. Remarkably, *beautiful* occurs only once. Another favorite, *fair*, here makes the first of 53 appearances in the 154 poems.

*Look in thy glass, and tell the face thou viewest
   Now is the time that face should form
      another;*
Whose fresh repair if now thou not renewest,
Thou dost beguile the world, unbless some mother.
For where is she so fair whose unear'd womb
Disdains the tillage of thy husbandry?
Or who is he so fond will be the tomb
Of his self-love, to stop posterity?
Thou art thy mother's glass, and she in thee
Calls back the lovely April of her prime;
So thou through windows of thine age shall see,
Despite of wrinkles this thy golden time.
   But if thou live, remember'd not to be,
   Die single, and thine image dies with thee.

SIRE A MIRRORING CHILD!

LOOK IN THE MIRROR and tell the face you see there that it's time to fashion another face. If you don't repair the present situation by renewing that image, you will cheat the world, and leave some mother unblessed.

For where is the woman so disdainfully beautiful that her virginal womb would reject the sowing of your seed? And where is the man so foolish that he would be the tomb of his own self-regard, and annul his own future?

You are your mother's mirror. In you she recalls the lovely April of her prime. No matter how wrinkled you get, through the windows of your aging eyes you too could revisit these, your golden years.

But if your life's goal is to end up forgotten, die single and let your looks perish with you.

Note: Ls1, 9: for *glass* see S103. / L5: *uneared*: unproductive (like corn). W.S. used this word in dedicating *Venus and Adonis* to H.W. / Since these early sonnets stress the passing of gifts from father to son, the mention of a mother is surprising. Did this Youth notably resemble his? Eager for grandmotherhood, did she subsidize these first 17 sonnets? / L10: in the calendar of the *Sonnets*, only April, May, June, and December are mentioned. / L10: *lovely*: the first of 8 appearances.

*U*nthrifty loveliness, why dost thou spend
  Upon thyself thy beauty's legacy?
Nature's bequest gives nothing, but doth lend,
And being frank, she lends to those are free.
Then, beauteous niggard, why dost thou abuse
The bounteous largess given thee to give?
Profitless usurer, why dost thou use
So great a sum of sums, yet canst not live?
For having traffic with thyself alone,
Thou of thyself thy sweet self dost deceive.
Then how, when Nature calls thee to be gone,
What acceptable Audit canst thou leave?
    Thy unus'd beauty must be tomb'd with thee,
    Which, used, lives th'executor to be.

FREELY YOU HAVE RECEIVED; FREELY GIVE.

—*Matthew* 10:8

YOU ARE A WASTEFUL loveliness. Why do you spend the legacy of your beauty on yourself alone? Nature's bequests are not permanent, but merely lent. Generous herself, nature would lend to those who are free-spenders.

Why then, lovely miser, do you abuse the rich gifts that were given to you to give away? Unprofitable banker, why do you use up such a sum of wealth without making an investment in the future? Doing business with yourself alone, you are cheating yourself of your own sweet self.

When nature terminates your contract, how will you be able to leave an acceptable audit? Your uninvested beauty must then be buried with you. If you had invested it, you would have left behind a living executor.

Note: L9: *traffic with thyself alone*: these early sonnets make several oblique references to self-pleasuring. / L10: in the very first sonnet we met one of the *Sonnets'* favorite adjectives, *sweet*. (The earliest reference to W.S.'s sonnets called them "sugred.") Here we meet another of its 55 usages. Other top compliments are *fair* (43 times), *true* (38), *best* (22), and *dear* (22).

5

Those hours, that with gentle work did frame
The lovely gaze where every eye doth dwell
Will play the tyrants to the very same
And that unfair which fairly doth excel;
For never-resting time leads summer on
To hideous winter, and confounds him there;
Sap check'd with frost, and lusty leaves quite gone,
Beauty o'ersnow'd and bareness everywhere:
Then were not summer's distillation left,
A liquid prisoner pent in walls of glass,
Beauty's effect with beauty were bereft,
Nor it, nor no remembrance what it was:
*   But flowers distill'd, though they with winter meet,*
*   Leese but their show; their substance still lives sweet.*

PERFUME: SUMMER'S SAVIOR

IT WAS THE GENTLE passage of time that produced those lovely looks of yours now captivating every eye. But the same march of the hours will turn destructive, and take the fairness away from the features which now excel in it.

Relentless time will turn summer into hideous winter and kill its graces. Frost will choke the sap; vigorous leaves will fall; snow will hide every charm; and all will be bare.

Thus, unless some of summer's beauty were distilled in the form of perfume—*a liquid prisoner pent in walls of glass*—loveliness and its effects would be lost, leaving neither themselves nor any sensual memories.

Though winter overtakes them, flowers lose but their outward show. Through distillation their sweet essence lingers on.

Note: This sonnet is unusual in its lack of both an "I" and a "thou." / L3: *unfair*: a verb, like deface. / L13: *leese*: release, lose. / L5: Repeated here as one of 70 instances, *time* is the 20th word of the entire sonnet sequence. *Beauty* is the 9th word, *die* the 12th, *decease* the 21st, and *memory* the 27th. In the very first of *Shakespeare's Sonnets*, then, almost all the sonnets' major themes announce themselves: beauty, time, death, and memory. Only *love* and *poetry* await their entrance. / The next sonnet carries on the argument with its opening *Then*.

6

*T*hen let not winter's ragged hand deface
    In thee thy summer, ere thou be distill'd:
Make sweet some vial; treasure thou some place
With beauty's treasure, ere it be self-kill'd.
That use is not forbidden usury,
Which happies those that pay the willing loan;
That's for thyself to breed another thee,
Or ten times happier, be it ten for one;
Ten times thyself were happier than thou art,
If ten of thine ten times refigur'd thee:
Then what could death do if thou shouldst depart,
Leaving thee living in posterity?
    Be not self-will'd, for thou art much too fair
    To be death's conquest and make worms thine heir.

YOUR CHILD,
YOUR FRAGRANCE

DON'T LET WINTER'S wasting hand deface
your summer self before your perfume is distilled.
Sweeten some vessel; loan to some womb the
treasure of your beauty, before you squander it
completely.

The return on your loan will not be a case of
sinful usury, for it will please her who repays it
through childbirth.

It's your duty to produce another you—or
produce ten more and make yourself ten times
happier. Then what total disaster could death
impose, if you leave this world while living on in
your posterity?

Please don't be so self-absorbed. You are much
too comely to be utterly consumed by death, and
make worms your only legatees.

Note: The son of a mother with six siblings, W.S. himself was the third of eight
children—the first son, and the first child to survive infancy; only his sister
Joan outlived him. Her descendants still survive. / L6: *happies*: a verb: rejoices.
/ In the previous sonnet, *summer* appears for the first of 21 times. In this one,
winter debuts for the first of 8 mentionings. *Spring* gets 5 notices; *autumn*
garners 2.

7

*L*o! in the orient when the gracious light
   Lifts up his burning head, each under eye
Doth homage to his new-appearing sight,
Serving with looks his sacred majesty;
And having climb'd the steep-up heavenly hill,
Resembling strong youth in his middle age,
Yet mortal looks adore his beauty still,
Attending on his golden pilgrimage;
But when from highmost pitch, with weary car,
Like feeble age, he reeleth from the day,
The eyes, 'fore duteous, now converted are
From his low tract, and look another way:
   So thou, thyself outgoing in thy noon,
   Unlook'd on diest, unless thou get a son.

SON WILL SAVE SUN

SEE HOW IN THE EAST the gracious sun lifts up its fiery head. Then all earthly eyes praise its fresh appearance, honoring with their gazes its sacred majesty.

In midday the sun keeps climbing the steep hill of heaven like a strong youth in his prime. Mortals continue to worship its beauty and follow it on its golden pilgrimage.

But when, like a feeble elder, the sun in its weary chariot declines from the zenith, eyes once worshipful turn from its low path and look elsewhere.

Likewise, you are now squandering your noontime, and will die unregarded if you don't beget a son.

Note: L2: *his burning head*: until about 1600, *its* was not in common use as a possessive pronoun. / L12: People admire sunsets too, but the poem presumably supposes a later time, when all the glory is gone. / Ls2, 11: here are two of 96 sonnet *eyes*. The first mention of the beloved's eyes was in S1. The heart is the next most cited body part in *Shakespeare's Sonnets* (61), then *face* (21), *tongue* (20), and *hand* (19). In lesser and diminishing frequency appear *brow, cheeks, blood, breast, lips, brains, flesh, bosom, ears, fingers, foot, hair, womb, eyelids, mouth, veins, jaw, neck, nerves, teeth,* and *voice*.

8

Music to hear, why hear'st thou music sadly?

Sweets with sweets war not, joy delights

in joy:

Why lov'st thou that which thou receiv'st not gladly,

Or else receiv'st with pleasure thine annoy?

If the true concord of well-tuned sounds,

By unions married, do offend thine ear,

They do but sweetly chide thee, who confounds

In singleness the parts that thou shouldst bear.

Mark how one string, sweet husband to another,

Strikes each in each by mutual ordering;

Resembling sire and child and happy mother,

Who, all in one, one pleasing note do sing:

Whose speechless song, being many, seeming one,

Sings this to thee: "Thou single wilt prove none."

HARMONY REBUKES BACHELORHOOD

YOU WHO ARE MUSIC TO MY EARS, why does music sadden you? Sweet things don't usually clash with one another, and joyous things cause mutual delight. Why then do you love music if you are not glad to hear it? Or rejoice in it if it upsets you?

Why does the harmony of well-tuned sounds, wed by their oneness, offend your ears? Because the harmony is chiding you. For by remaining unmarried you are betraying your part in life's concert.

Note how one string is like a sweet spouse to the other; each strikes its note in a mutual ordering—like a father, a child, and a happy mother. Altogether they produce one pleasing chord. Wordlessly these strings, both one and many, are singing this warning to you: "As a single man, you count for nothing."

Note: Likened here to a family of father, happy mother, and child, *music* makes the first of 6 sonnet appearances. Other family words in *Shakespeare's Sonnets*: *husband* (4), *father* (3), *sire* (1), *mother* (5), *widow* (3), *wife* (1), *child* (10), *babe* (4), *son* and *boy* (3 each), *home* (3), and *house* (1), *married* (2), and *marriage* (1). Gender words are *man* (27), *woman* (9), *mistress* (8), *maid* (4), *master* and *virgin* (1). There is no "brother," "sister," "girl" or "daughter"; no "family" or "wedding."

9

Is it for fear to wet a widow's eye
That thou consum'st thyself in single life?
Ah! if thou issueless shalt hap to die,
The world will wail thee like a makeless wife;
The world will be thy widow and still weep
That thou no form of thee hast left behind,
When every private widow well may keep,
By children's eyes her husband's shape in mind.
Look what an unthrift in the world doth spend
Shifts but his place, for still the world enjoys it;
But beauty's waste hath in the world an end,
And kept unus'd, the user so destroys it.

    No love toward others in that bosom sits
    That on himself such murd'rous shame commits.

YOU'LL LEAVE A WIDOW IN ANY CASE

IS THIS WHY you are burning yourself out as a bachelor—you don't want to leave behind a weeping widow? Alas, if you do die without offspring, the world will weep for you like a wife without a mate.

As your widow, the world will grieve that you left behind no image of yourself. Other widows can be reminded of their husbands by their children's eyes.

Think of this: the world can still enjoy the money a wastrel squanders because his wealth has merely changed hands. But the world loses wasted beauty forever. If the beauty isn't productive, the possessor destroys it.

There is no love for others in the heart of a man who commits such a shameful crime against himself.

Note: L5: in W.S.'s day, *still* often meant "always." / L13: *love*, which appears 164 times in the 154 sonnets, here makes its first appearance, unexpectedly delayed in poems about marriage and procreation. The following sonnet makes up for this delay by four uses of the word. All told, W.S.'s works speak of *love* some 2,200 times; variations of the word (e.g., *loved*) bring the total to about 3,100.

10

For shame deny that thou bear'st love to any,
 Who for thyself art so unprovident.
Grant, if thou wilt, thou art belov'd of many,
But that thou none lov'st is most evident;
For thou art so possessed with murd'rous hate
That 'gainst thyself thou stick'st not to conspire.
Seeking that beauteous roof to ruinate
Which to repair should be thy chief desire.
O change thy thought, that I may change my mind!
Shall hate be fairer lodged than gentle love?
Be as thy presence is, gracious and kind,
Or to thyself at least kind-hearted prove:
 Make thee another self for love of me,
 That beauty still may live in thine or thee.

PROCREATE FOR LOVE OF ME

YOU SHOULD SHAMEFULLY admit that you love no one, you who are so shortsighted about yourself. Granted, many people love you, but it is blindingly clear that you don't return the favor.

You are so possessed with life-killing disdain [against marriage] that you don't hesitate to conspire against yourself—striving to ruin that lovely mansion of your family heritage, when preserving and enlarging it should be your overmastering desire.

Please change your policy so that I may change my mind. Should a disdainful man have more attractive looks than a tender lover? Be as gracious and kind to others as your appearance argues that you are. Or at least be tender toward yourself.

For love of me, too, beget an heir, so that such beauty as yours can keep on living, either now in yourself or later in your offspring.

Note: L9: though "we" was the fourth word of S1, this is the first use of "I" in any form. / L9: also, "O" makes here the first of 50 appearances; it's the most frequent first word of the *Sonnets* (13 times; When, 10; How, 7). / L13: *for love of me*: a key development: the love between the poet and the Youth enters the scene. S15, L13 will balance the dynamic with *for love of you.*

11

As fast as thou shalt wane, so fast thou grow'st
In one of thine, from that which thou departest;
And that fresh blood which youngly thou bestow'st
Thou mayst call thine when thou from youth
convertest.
Herein lives wisdom, beauty and increase;
Without this, folly, age and cold decay:
If all were minded so, the times should cease
And threescore year would make the world away.
Let those whom Nature hath not made for store,
Harsh, featureless, and rude, barrenly perish:
Look whom she best endowed she gave the more;
Which bounteous gift thou shouldst in bounty cherish:
She carv'd thee for her seal, and meant thereby
Thou shouldst print more, not let that copy die.

YOU ARE NATURE'S SEAL. MAKE COPIES!

AS FAST AS YOU yourself fade away, just so fast will there grow in your child those very qualities that you are leaving behind. When you lose your youthfulness, you can claim as your own the fresh blood you gave him in your prime. By procreating you will gain wisdom, beauty, and growth; otherwise, you will reap folly, old age, and cold decay.

If everyone behaved like you, history would cease, and in sixty years the world would be depopulated. Intending no permanence for them, Nature made some people harsh, unlovely, and unfinished. Let them perish without issue.

Remember: Nature wants more from those she has most generously endowed. You should manage such plentiful gifts generously. She made you her seal, and intended that additional copies should keep that mold from perishing.

Note: L9: *nature*, a major force in the *Sonnets*, is here mentioned for the first of 16 times. Aspects of nature are copiously cited: *heavens* (22), *sun* (13), *earth* (11), *stars* (8), *clouds* (6), *sea* and *water* (5 each), *rain*, *moon*, and *ocean* (3 each), *eclipses* (2), *twilight*, *sunset*, *sky*, and *snow* (1 each). There is no "dawn" or "dusk."

When I do count the clock that tells the time,
And see the brave day sunk in hideous night,
When I behold the violet past prime,
And sable curls all silver'd o'er with white,
When lofty trees I see barren of leaves,
Which erst from heat did canopy the herd,
And summer's green all girded up in sheaves
Borne on the bier with white and bristly beard,
Then of thy beauty do I question make
Since sweets and beauties do themselves forsake,
That thou among the wastes of time must go,
And die as fast as they see others grow,

    And nothing 'gainst Time's scythe can make defence
    Save breed, to brave him when he takes thee hence.

I SEE YOUR FADING EVERYWHERE

A VARIETY OF THINGS remind me that your beauty is passing away: the chimes of a clock; the splendid day sinking into hideous night; a violet past its prime; curls once black, silvered into white; lofty trees stripped of the leaves that used to shadow the herd from the heat; summer's once-green crops bound in sheaves and carted away white and bristly.

All these things remind me that you too will be wasted by Time—since persons sweet and beautiful all lose their charms in the end. They die down as swiftly as they see their replacements growing up.

It's clear to me that nothing can save you from Time's harvesting scythe except the breeding of issue who can thumb their noses at Time when he carries you off.

Note: The lines of this clean-cut sonnet swing inexorably, like a slicing pendulum. This 12th sonnet starts out with a clock, which has 12 numbers. Coincidence? See S60. / Obsessed with the rush of time, the *Sonnets* speak of *clocks* (2), *minutes* (4), *hours* (6), *nights* (26), *days* (44), *week* (1), *years* (7), *morning* (4), *evening* (2), *noon*, *twilight*, and *sunset* (1 each). *Now* occurs 45 times; *today* and *tomorrow* thrice each. There is no "yesterday."

13

O that you were yourself! but, love, you are
 No longer yours than you yourself here live:
Against this coming end you should prepare,
And your sweet semblance to some other give:
So should that beauty which you hold in lease
Find no determination; then you were
Yourself again, after yourself's decease,
When your sweet issue your sweet form should bear.
Who lets so fair a house fall to decay,
Which husbandry in honour might uphold
Against the stormy gusts of winter's day
And barren rage of death's eternal cold?
    O none but unthrifts. Dear my love, you know
    You had a father: let your son say so.

YOU HAD A FATHER;
LET YOUR SON SAY SO

O MY BELOVED, I wish that you would always be you! But you possess yourself only as long as you live here on earth. So, prepare against your coming death by imprinting your charming likeness on someone else.

That way, the beauty that you now lease will not be terminated. For after your demise, you will enjoy a fresh incarnation: it will come from the sweet resemblance that your offspring will bear to your own sweet self.

What master would let his stately mansion fall into decay when his diligence could preserve its honor against the stormy gusts of winter's day, and against the life-killing fury of death's eternal cold? Only a wasteful soul would behave that way. Oh my dear love, you had a father. Beget a son who can say the same.

Note: Here for the first time *thou* becomes *you* (17 times!). The variation might have been based merely on considerations of sound. The old distinction between the intimate *thou* and the general *you* was fading in England at this time. / Here also, in Ls1, 13, is a truly seismic change: for the first time, the poet declares his love for the Youth. / L13: here is the first use of *dear*, which, unsurprisingly, makes 20 more appearances. *Beloved* is used 5 times, once as a noun. / L14: eight-year-old H.W. became an Earl upon his father's death in 1581. He was about 20 when the Bard dedicated *Venus and Adonis* to him, 21 when *The Rape of Lucrece* was so dedicated.

SONNET 13

14

*N*ot from the stars do I my judgement
pluck,

And yet methinks I have astronomy,

But not to tell of good or evil luck,

Of plagues, of dearths, or seasons' quality;

Nor can I fortune to brief minutes tell,

Pointing to each his thunder, rain, and wind,

Or say with princes if it shall go well

By oft predict that I in heaven find:

But from thine eyes my knowledge I derive,

And, constant stars, in them I read such art

As Truth and beauty shall together thrive,

If from thyself to store thou wouldst convert:

    Or else of thee this I prognosticate:

    Thy end is truth's and beauty's doom and date.

YOUR EYES MAKE ME AN ASTROLOGER

I DON'T DERIVE my knowledge from the stars. Yet I am an astrologer of sorts. Not that I predict good or bad luck, plagues, famines, or the weather.

I can't foretell, to the split second, when thunder, rain, or wind will come. Nor can I, through some prophetic celestial sign, reveal whether things shall go well with rulers.

I get my information from those constant stars, which are your eyes. There I see such power as would keep both truth and beauty flourishing together—if only you would transform yourself into a surplus. I "predict" that, if you don't, truth and beauty are doomed, and timed to expire with you.

Note: Ls 11, 14: *truth and beauty* here make their first of many twinned appearances. Along with goodness, they formed a well-known philosophical triad. *Truth* appears 25 times in the *Sonnets*, and *beauty* 84 times (20 times already!). In the *Sonnets*, *truth* is an inward quality, like integrity and honesty; *beauty*, an outward quality. Sometimes the poet speaks of the Youth as the heavenly model of ideal *Truth* and *Beauty*, whence the final line of this sonnet. As rhymes, *youth* and *truth* invariably appear together. (See Ss 37, 41, 54, 60, 110, and 138.)

15

hen I consider every thing that grows
Holds in perfection but a little moment,
That this huge stage presenteth nought but shows
Whereon the stars in secret influence comment;
When I perceive that men as plants increase,
Cheered and checked even by the self-same sky,
Vaunt in their youthful sap, at height decrease,
And wear their brave state out of memory;
Then the conceit of this inconstant stay
Sets you most rich in youth before my sight,
Where wasteful Time debateth with Decay,
To change your day of youth to sullied night;
    And all in war with Time for love of you,
    As he takes from you, I engraft you new.

NOTHING GOLD CAN STAY, SAVE GOLDEN WORDS

WHEN I CONSIDER how every growing thing has but one brief shining moment of perfection, history seems but a vast stage featuring nothing but plays. The audience for these shows is the stars, whose critical role in these dramas remains mysterious.

Men are like plants: they are nurtured and frustrated by the very same heavens. Thus men glory in their young juices, start to wither at their prime, and march their glowing gifts into oblivion.

This perception of inconstancy makes your youthfulness loom most precious in my eyes, for wasteful Time is consorting with Decay to bring your day of pure youth stained into night.

For love of you I wage total war on Time: while it is diminishing your youth, I will be grafting you onto something new.

Note: Another key development: here and in the next two sonnets appear the first references to the poet's desire to preserve his young friend through poetry. This theme occurs in a dozen sonnets. Poetry itself is featured in another two dozen. / L1: *consider* is the perfect word, since it means "being with the stars" (cum/sidera). The opening words of this sonnet echo in John Milton's classic sonnet on his blindness: "When I consider how my light is spent..."

16

*B*ut wherefore do not you a mightier way
  Make war upon this bloody tyrant, Time?
And fortify yourself in your decay
With means more blessed than my barren rhyme?
Now stand you on the top of happy hours,
And many maiden gardens, yet unset,
With virtuous wish would bear your living flowers,
Much liker than your painted counterfeit:
So should the lines of life that life repair,
Which this Time's pencil, or my pupil pen,
Neither in inward worth nor outward fair,
Can make you live yourself in eyes of men.
    To give away yourself, keeps yourself still,
    And you must live, drawn by your own sweet skill.

ADVICE FOR HAPPY HOURS

DESPITE MY POETIC PLANS, why don't you wield an even more powerful weapon in making war against the bloody tyranny of Time? Why don't you protect yourself against your own decay by a more blessed means than my infertile verses?

You are standing now at the top of happy hours, and many a virtuous maiden, as yet unseeded, would gladly be the garden that bore your flower children. These would capture your likeness much better than any image painted with oil or words.

Thus should bloodlines preserve that life of yours and keep you alive in the eyes of men. For your inward or outward beauty cannot be forever maintained by Time's brush or my novice pen.

By giving yourself in procreation, you preserve yourself. And survive you must if you create your own living image.

Note: L4: the speaker here admits what the previous sonnets have shown: he is a rhymer. Swiftly changing his tune, though, he is already doubting whether his poems can confer immortality. Maybe he didn't want the Youth to find in them an excuse for childlessness. / L11: *worth* is a frequent sonnet subject, occurring 30 times. There are 4 *costs*, but no "price" or "value."

17

Who will believe my verse in time to come
If it were filled with your most high deserts?
Though yet, heaven knows, it is but as a tomb
Which hides your life, and shows not half your parts.
If I could write the beauty of your eyes
And in fresh numbers number all your graces,
The age to come would say, "This poet lies;
Such heavenly touches ne'er touched earthly faces."
So should my papers, yellowed with their age,
Be scorned, like old men of less truth than tongue,
And your true rights be termed a poet's rage
And stretched metre of an antique song:
    But were some child of yours alive that time,
    You should live twice, in it, and in my rhyme.

HOW COULD THEY BELIEVE ME?

—*Jerome Kern*

WHO IN THE FUTURE would believe my poems
if they were full of the lofty praises you deserve?
Heaven knows, however, that thus far my verses are
like a tomb that hides the reality, an epitaph that
re-counts not even half your merits.

If I could describe the beauty of your eyes, or list
all your charms in fresh verses, future readers would
say: "This poet lies—such divine qualities never
shone in a human face."

Thus would my manuscript, yellowed with age,
be dismissed like an old man who has more tongue
than truth. Your worthy praises would be deemed
a poet's frenzy, aping the bloated rhetoric of an
ancient eulogy.

But if some offspring of yours were alive at
that time, you would enjoy a double life: in your
descendant and in my poetry.

Note: This is the last sonnet explicitly urging the Youth to procreate. / L10: a
major theme of the *Sonnets* is *truth,* which occurs 25 times; *true* (37); *untrue*
(2); *false* (20); *falsehood* (2); *lie* (9); *deceive* (5) (but no "deceit"). / L10: poetry is
very fond of comparisons: explicit (simile) or implicit (metaphor). Two sonnets
begin with *Like*; there are 32 other usages of the word. One of the most famous
comparisons follows.

Shall I compare thee to a summer's day?
    Thou art more lovely and more temperate:
Rough winds do shake the darling buds of May,
And summer's lease hath all too short a date;
Sometime too hot the eye of heaven shines,
And often is his gold complexion dimmed;
And every fair from fair sometime declines,
By chance or nature's changing course untrimmed:
But thy eternal summer shall not fade,
Nor lose possession of that fair thou ow'st,
Nor shall Death brag thou wander'st in his shade,
When in eternal lines to time thou grow'st;
    So long as men can breathe or eyes can see,
    So long lives this, and this gives life to thee.

YOUR INCOMPARABLE, ENDLESS SUMMER

SHALL I LIKEN YOU to a summery day? You are more winsome and gentle than that, for winds can roughen up the beloved blossoms of May, and summer lasts for all too short a spell.

Besides, at times the sun stares down with too hot an eye; and its gold complexion often gets clouded over. Thus everything fair sometimes loses its fairness. Chance or nature's cycle of changes lessens every charm.

But your everlasting summer will not fade, nor will it lose the beauty that is yours. Since these undying lines will preserve you throughout time, death will not be able to brag that you wander utterly shrouded in his shadows.

As long as human beings can breathe and eyes can read, this poem will live and give life to you.

Note: Perfect in its form, S18 is the favorite of many. / L10 could refer to the beauty the young man possesses (*ow'st*=owns); or to the debt he "owes" to Death. / The poet makes May part of summer. In his day May was warmer, since the unreformed English calendar was about two weeks behind nature's schedule. / In the 1998 movie *Shakespeare in Love*, the poet dashes off S18 for Gwyneth Paltrow, definitely a woman. See S29 for book titles mined from this sonnet.

19

Devouring Time, blunt thou the lion's paws,
And make the earth devour her own sweet
brood;
Pluck the keen teeth from the fierce tiger's jaws,
And burn the long-lived phoenix in her blood;
Make glad and sorry seasons as thou fleet'st,
And do whate'er thou wilt, swift-footed Time,
To the wide world and all her fading sweets;
But I forbid thee one most heinous crime:
O carve not with thy hours my love's fair brow,
Nor draw no lines there with thine antique pen;
Him in thy course untainted do allow
For beauty's pattern to succeeding men.
   Yet do thy worst, old Time: despite thy wrong,
   My love shall in my verse ever live young.

TO TIME: YES AND
A USELESS NO

DO YOUR WORST, O ravenous Time: blunt the
lion's paw; make the burying earth devour its own
sweet human brood; pluck out the teeth from the
fierce tiger's jaws; burn the long-lived Phoenix
bird in her own blood forever; make the seasons
happy or sad as you race on; do whatever you want,
fleet-footed Time, to the wide world and all its
decaying delights.

But I forbid you one most monstrous crime: do
not carve traces of your ticking on my lover's lovely
brow; draw no wrinkles there with your antiquating
pen. As you pass, let him remain unspoiled as a
model of beauty for men of future time.

All right—do your worst, old Time. Despite your
crimes, my love and my beloved will live forever
young in my poetry.

Note: L4: It was only by totally consuming itself by fire every 500 years that the
mythical Arabian bird, the Phoenix, could renew its life cycle. A 67-line love
song, *The Phoenix and the Turtle*, published in 1601, was ascribed to W.S. and
is generally believed to be authentic. / L8: Time's crime is not just the death of
one handsome man, but its (imagined) destruction of the very mold of Male
Beauty. / In the spirit of this sonnet, Abraham Lincoln once spoke of "time's
silent artillery."

20

A woman's face with Nature's own hand painted

Hast thou, the Master Mistress of my passion;

A woman's gentle heart, but not acquainted

With shifting change, as is false women's fashion;

An eye more bright than theirs, less false in rolling,

Gilding the object whereupon it gazeth;

A man in hue, all Hues *in his controlling,*

Which steals men's eyes and women's souls amazeth.

And for a woman wert thou first created;

Till Nature as she wrought thee fell a-doting,

And by addition me of thee defeated,

By adding one thing to my purpose nothing.

   But since she prick'd thee out for women's pleasure,

   Mine be thy love and thy love's use their treasure.

A CLASSIC OF GENDER CONFUSION

YOU ARE BOTH Master and Mistress of my passion. Yours is a woman's face, painted by Nature's own hand. You also have a gentle heart, though not, in the style of untrue women, a fickle one.

Gilding whatever they look on, your eyes are brighter than women's, less false in their flirtations. A man in form, you master the traits of both sexes. Such a person steals men's eyes, and spellbinds the souls of women.

In the womb you began as a woman, until lady Nature fell for you, and defeated me of a mistress by adding something useless to such a role. Yes, she pronged you out for women's ecstasy. So let your love be mine, while you devote love's instrument to enrich their treasuries.

Note: This sonnet is one of the most discussed brief pieces in all of literature. L7: the word *Hues—Hews* in the original—is capitalized and italicized. Is this *H*/enry *E*/arl *W*/riothesley *S*/outhampton? / L13: A *prick* was any sharp, pointed object, or even a puncture point made next to a listed name. It easily became a slang word for the male organ. Likewise, *treasure* and *treasury* were synonyms for the female organs. / Uniquely but fittingly, this sonnet uses only feminine rhymes—words ending "weakly" on an unaccented syllable.

21

So is it not with me as with that Muse
Stirr'd by a painted beauty to his verse,
Who heaven itself for ornament doth use,
And every fair with his fair doth rehearse,
Making a couplement of proud compare
With sun and moon, with earth and sea's rich gems,
With April's first-born flowers, and all things rare
That heaven's air in this huge rondure hems.
O let me, true in love, but truly write,
And then believe me, my love is as fair
As any mother's child, though not so bright
As those gold candles fix'd in heaven's air:

> *Let them say more that like of hearsay well;*
> *I will not praise that purpose not to sell.*

DOWN WITH HYPE THAT SELLS

I AM NOT LIKE the bemused poet who, when some dolled-up beauty inspires him to versify, decorates his poems with images plucked from the very heavens.

He links his subject with everything else beautiful, associating his beloved with the sun, the moon, the earth, the sea's rich hidden gems, with April's newborn flowers, with everything rare that the skies enclose in this huge, round world.

Let me be true in my loving, but still write truly. Then believe me when I say that my beloved is as lovely as any mother's child, though not quite so bright as those golden candles fixed in the night sky.

Those poets who admire the tributes given to reputed beauties of the past—let them use more extravagant words. I refuse to praise as though my purpose were to increase sales through extravagance.

Note: With this sonnet the Muses enter the scene, along with the issue of competing poetic theories. The Muses were nine sister goddesses of Greek mythology, who presided over song, poetry, art, and science. (They nest in the words *music, museum, mosaic, amuse,* and *bemuse.*) The lyre-playing Erato ("the Beloved") was usually the Muse of love poetry. The *Sonnets* give no name to their Muse. Sometime she seems to dwell in the poet, sometimes in the beloved, inspiringly.

22

y glass shall not persuade me I am old,
So long as youth and thou are of one date,
But when in thee time's furrows I behold,
Then look I death my days should expiate;
For all that beauty that doth cover thee
Is but the seemly raiment of my heart,
Which in thy breast doth live, as thine in me.
How can I then be elder than thou art?
O therefore, love, be of thyself so wary
As I not for myself but for thee will,
Bearing thy heart, which I will keep so chary
As tender nurse her babe from faring ill.

　　Presume not on thy heart when mine is slain;
　　Thou gav'st me thine, not to give back again.

YOUR YOUTH KEEPS ME YOUNG

MY MIRROR WILL NOT convince me that I am old, so long as you and youth are contemporaries. But when I first detect on you the wrinkles of time, then I will start preparing to pay my debt to death.

For all the loveliness that clothes you is but the proper vesture of my heart—a heart that lives in your breast, as yours does in mine. How then can I be older than you?

Therefore, my beloved, take care of yourself. I will do the same—not for myself, but for your sake. For I carry your heart, and I will guard it as carefully as a tender nurse who keeps her babe from harm.

One warning, though: do not presume to regain your heart when mine has stopped. True, you gave it to me. But it is a gift which cannot be returned.

Note: S22 gives a fanciful warning to the so-called "Fair Youth": Don't slay me with rejection, because, if you do, you won't get your heart back. The addressee of the *Sonnets* is often called *fair*, but *Youth* only once (S54), and never "Fair Youth" (though he is traditionally so-called). He is often called *friend*, but *fair friend* (S104) only once. / L4: Though death hovers over all of the *Sonnets*, this one uses the word itself in the first of 16 explicit mentions. The *Sonnets* also speak of *youth* (16), *young* (5), *youthful* (2), *old* (22), *age* (15), *dead* (16), *(a)live* (29), and *life* (24).

23

As an unperfect actor on the stage,
Who with his fear is put besides his part,
Or some fierce thing replete with too much rage,
Whose strength's abundance weakens his own heart;
So I, for fear of trust, forget to say
The perfect ceremony of love's rite,
And in mine own love's strength seem to decay,
O'ercharged with burden of mine own love's might.
O let my books be then the eloquence
And dumb presagers of my speaking breast,
Who plead for love, and look for recompense,
More than that tongue that more hath more expressed.
  O learn to read what silent love hath writ:
  To hear with eyes belongs to love's fine wit.

LET YOUR EYES HEAR BETWEEN MY LINES

I AM LIKE a bumbling actor whose stage fright makes him forget his lines. For, fearing to trust myself, I forget to voice perfectly the expected words of love.

I am like a fierce beast too much enraged, whose very strength impedes him. Overburdened by the might of my affections, I seem to be growing weaker in the power of my love.

Let my looks, then, be my eloquence. Let them be the imperfect intimations of what my heart is saying. They plead on behalf of love, and long for a return of love—more than any tongue that has more often said more.

Learn to read what unspoken love has written in my expressions. For hearing with the eyes is part of love's privileged way of knowing.

Note: The poet was also an actor, a playwright, and a shareholder who knew all about the stage. He was probably the world's first total man of the theater. Traveling troupes are known to have performed in young Shakespeare's village, and such a group may well have sparked his love for the theater. / L9: the original *books* may have been a misprint for "looks." / L12: a triad of *mores*; the wordy tongue may have belonged to a rival for the beloved's patronage.

24

Mine eye hath played the painter and hath steeled

Thy beauty's form in table of my heart;

My body is the frame wherein 'tis held,

And perspective it is best painter's art.

For through the painter must you see his skill

To find where your true image pictured lies,

Which in my bosom's shop is hanging still,

That hath his windows glazed with thine eyes.

Now see what good turns eyes for eyes have done:

Mine eyes have drawn thy shape, and thine for me

Are windows to my breast, wherethrough the sun

Delights to peep, to gaze therein on thee.

　　Yet eyes this cunning want to grace their art,

　　They draw but what they see, know not the heart.

EYES THAT DO EACH OTHER FAVORS

MY EYES HAVE PLAYED the painter, and etched your lovely shape on the canvas of my heart. My body is thus the frame of your image, rendered with that skill of perspective which the best artists possess.

It is by peering through the painter in me that you will realize my talent, and find where your true likeness is pictured. It is a portrait always hanging in my heart's shop, whose windows are also reflecting your eyes.

See now what favors our eyes have done for each other: I have used mine to draw your image; reflecting me, your eyes are the windows to my breast within. [Like a window-shopper], the sun loves to peep through my eyes to study the you inside me.

Still, eyes lack one skill to perfect their artistry: they draw but what they see, but cannot see the heart.

Note: S24 is among the most difficult. The main dynamic is two people gazing into each other's mirroring eyes. / The dashing Earl of Southampton (H.W.), with his blue eyes and dark auburn hair, was one of the most painted men of his time. Some 50 portraits of him survive.

*L*et those who are in favour with their stars
  Of public honour and proud titles boast,
Whilst I, whom fortune of such triumph bars,
Unlooked for joy in that I honour most.
Great princes' favourites their fair leaves spread
But as the marigold at the sun's eye,
And in themselves their pride lies buried,
For at a frown they in their glory die.
The painful warrior famoused for worth,
After a thousand victories once foil'd,
Is from the book of honour razed quite,
And all the rest forgot for which he toil'd:
  Then happy I, that love and am belov'd
  Where I may not remove, nor be remov'd.

WHERE PRINCES DO NOT PAUPERIZE

LET THOSE WHO are lucky in their stars brag about their public honors and proud titles. Fate denies me such triumphs, yet I unexpectedly rejoice in the man I honor most.

The favorites of powerful princes spread their lovely leaves as does the marigold in the sunshine. But these favorites are the potential tombs of their own pride, for a mere frown can kill their glory.

Though celebrated for his fighting and a thousand victories, the wounded warrior need undergo but one defeat, and his name is utterly erased from the book of honor. All that he struggled for becomes forgotten.

How fortunate I am! For I love and am beloved in a court where no prince replaces, and no favorite is replaced.

Note: Though the Sonnets make no mention of "providence," "God's Will," or "destiny," there are nine references to fortune, and one each to fate, luck, and chance. / L9: in the original printing, this line ends with worth, which, uniquely, does not rhyme with its partner (L11). Editors sometimes replace worth with "fight" or "might." No one seems inclined to replace quite with a word rhyming with worth.

26

Lord of my love, to whom in vassalage
　Thy merit hath my duty strongly knit,
To thee I send this written embassage,
To witness duty, not to show my wit;
Duty so great, which wit so poor as mine
May make seem bare, in wanting words to show it,
But that I hope some good conceit of thine
In thy soul's thought, all naked, will bestow it,
Till whatsoever star that guides my moving
Points on me graciously with fair aspect,
And puts apparel on my tatter'd loving,
To show me worthy of thy sweet respect:
　　Then may I dare to boast how I do love thee,
　　Till then, not show my head where thou mayst
prove me.

MY POEMS ARE NOT
YET WORTHY OF YOU

YOU ARE THE LORD of my loving, and your merits have strongly bound me to you as your dutiful vassal. These verses which I mail to you are mere ambassadors—to acknowledge my duty, not to display my skill. My allegiance is rich enough. My talents are so poor, however, that my loyalty may seem quite threadbare, since I lack the words to express it.

My hope is that in your transparent thoughtfulness you will clothe my words with some enriching interpretation. May this be the case until whatever star guides my poetic growth shines on me with a fully gracious gaze. Then may this star lavishly robe my tattered love, so that I become worthy of your sweet regard.

When that happens I will dare to say how much I love you. Till then, I'll not risk exposing myself openly to your critiquing.

Note: Observe how this first "mail" sonnet strikingly echoes W.S.'s dedication of *The Rape of Lucrece* to H.W.: "The *love* I dedicate to your *lord*ship is without end…Were my *worth* greater, my *duty* [twice in the dedication, thrice in the sonnet] would *show* greater" (see S120). Was this sonnet sent along with the 1594 dedication? / L4's *wit* means, as it does 7 times elsewhere, sharp intelligence, not wittiness. The poet here wittily plays on wit and witness.

27

Weary with toil, I haste me to my bed,
   The dear repose for limbs with travel
tired,
But then begins a journey in my head
To work my mind, when body's work's expired;
For then my thoughts—from far where I abide—
Intend a zealous pilgrimage to thee,
And keep my drooping eyelids open wide,
Looking on darkness which the blind do see;
Save that my soul's imaginary sight
Presents thy shadow to my sightless view,
Which, like a jewel hung in ghastly night
Makes black night beauteous, and her old face new.
   Lo! thus, by day my limbs, by night my mind,
   For thee, and for myself, no quiet find.

NIGHT AND DAY,
YOU ARE THE ONE
—COLE PORTER

EXHAUSTED WITH EFFORT, I hasten to my bed, the precious resting place for travel-weary limbs. But then I start a journey in my head, setting my mind to work just when my body's work is done. At once my thoughts embark on a zealous pilgrimage to you, who are far from where I lodge.

These thoughts prop my drooping eyelids open wide, keep them looking on that darkness which blind eyes see—except that my soul's imagination conjures up your shape before my sightless gaze. That vision is like a jeweled planet hanging in the ghostly night, making black night beautiful and its wizened features youthful.

Thus it is that my limbs find no peace by day, nor my mind by night. I find repose neither for my thoughts of you, nor for myself.

Note: Following the first "mail" sonnet, S27 inaugurates the first set of travel sonnets, and the first instance of insomnia. *Shakespeare's Sonnets* have *dreams* (4), *sleep* (6), and a single *slumber*. There are three *beds* and six *darks*. / This one sonnet contains a number of key, related words often used elsewhere: *head* (6), *mind* (16), *soul* (14), and *thought* (36). There are, in addition, 12 references to *spirit*, and 15 to *think*.

28

*H*ow can I then return in happy plight
    That am debarred the benefit of rest?
When day's oppression is not eased by night,
But day by night, and night by day, oppressed;
And each, though enemies to either's reign,
Do in consent shake hands to torture me,
The one by toil, the other to complain
How far I toil, still farther off from thee.
I tell the day, to please him, thou art bright
And dost him grace when clouds do blot the heaven;
So flatter I the swart-complexioned night,
When sparkling stars twire not thou gild'st the even.
    But day doth daily draw my sorrows longer,
    And night doth nightly make grief's length seem
stronger.

STRANGE BEDFELLOWS TORTURE ME

HOW CAN I get out of bed with a smile on my face when I can't get a decent night's sleep—when the weight of day is not relieved by night, but rather day is wearied by night, and night by day?

Normally these two kingdoms war on each other. But now they shake hands and both agree to torture me. Day tortures me with work; night, by keeping me awake with the thought that my work takes me ever farther from you.

To please the day I tell it that when skies are cloudy your brightness graciously saves the day. I likewise flatter the black-complexioned night by saying that when no stars twinkle your brightness gilds the darkness.

But it's no use: day protracts my sorrows daily, and every night the night makes the weight of my griefs seem heavier.

Note: Why should *Day* and *Night* conspire to torture the poet in this rather tortuous sonnet? Perhaps somehow they too feel exiled from the Fair Youth, and forgotten by him. They are therefore venting their rage on his friend. That's why the friend tries to placate these two planetary Spirits by fancifully maintaining that the absent Youth is remembering them and even personally guarding their reputations.

29

_**W**hen, in disgrace with Fortune and
men's eyes,_

I all alone beweep my outcast state,

And trouble deaf heaven with my bootless cries,

And look upon myself and curse my fate,

Wishing me like to one more rich in hope,

Featured like him, like him with friends possessed,

Desiring this man's art, and that man's scope,

With what I most enjoy contented least;

Yet in these thoughts myself almost despising,

Haply I think on thee, and then my state

Like to the lark at break of day arising

From sullen earth, sings hymns at heaven's gate;

_For thy sweet love remember'd such wealth
brings_

That then I scorn to change my state with kings.

THE THOUGHT OF YOU RIGHTS EVERY WRONG

SOMETIMES, WHEN I AM in the bad graces of good fortune and have lost the esteem of others, I find myself in utter loneliness. Then, shedding tears over my plight as an outcast, I badger deaf heaven with my useless prayers.

I gaze into the mirror and curse my fate. I wish I had someone else's richer prospects, or better looks, or more numerous friends. I wish I had this man's artistry, or that man's influence. My favorite delights please me least.

Yet, even in the midst of these almost self-hating thoughts, I sometimes happen to think of you. Then my state of mind becomes like the lark that rises from the sullen earth at daybreak and sings its hymns at the gate of heaven.

For when I remember your sweet love I feel so rich that I would treat with contempt the chance to trade places with a king.

Note: This much-beloved sonnet is "a carol to consolation." The singing lark is surrounded by despi/*sing* and ari/*sing*. Each of the final rhymes also "sing" indirectly: brings / kings. The poet's useless cries at deaf heaven are transformed into bird hymns at heaven's gate. / W.S.'s words provided titles for many other works of literature. At least 15 titles came from this sonnet (e.g., *Heaven's Gate*). S18 supplied 19 titles, 10 of which used *summer's lease*.

30

When to the sessions of sweet silent thought
   I summon up remembrance of things
      past,
I sigh the lack of many a thing I sought,
And with old woes new wail my dear time's waste;
Then can I drown an eye, unused to flow,
For precious friends hid in death's dateless night,
And weep afresh love's long since cancelled woe,
And moan the expense of many a vanished sight;
Then can I grieve at grievances foregone,
And heavily from woe to woe tell o'er
The sad account of fore-bemoaned moan,
Which I new pay as if not paid before.
   But if the while I think on thee, dear friend,
   All losses are restored, and sorrows end.

REMEMBRANCE OF THINGS PAST

SOMETIMES I WILL be enjoying a spell of quiet, mellow musing. But if memory stirs the ashes of the past, I start sighing for dreams unfulfilled, and revive afresh the old woes I felt for the waste of my priceless youth. My eyes, usually dry, can brim with tears for precious friends now shrouded in death's never-ending night.

I can weep anew from the pains of love long since forgotten, and bemoan the loss of many a vanished vision. I can grieve again for complaints I once dismissed, and repeat one by one the sorry list of grievances I've already lamented. These tax me again as though I hadn't already paid for them.

But if suddenly I think of you, dear friend, everything I lost feels restored, and every sorrow finally put to rest.

Note: This prize sonnet is oddly legalistic: court sessions, summoned witnesses, accounts reviewed and settled. / A phrase in L2 provided an inaccurate title for the English version of Marcel Proust's *À la recherche du temps perdu* (*In Search of Lost Time*). / Six sonnets contain *tears*; a few others, like this and the previous one, use synonyms: *weep* (3), *beweep, drown an eye, wet an eye*. S30 is truly woebegone, with 3 of the 14 sonnet *woes*, 3 of its 5 *moans*, 2 of its 7 *griefs*, 1 of its 7 *sorrows*, and 8 *sads*, and half its *sighs*. Still, *Shakespeare's Sonnets* have no "sadness" or "happiness"! But *happy* has 15 appearances.

31

*T*hy bosom is endeared with all hearts,
  Which I by lacking have supposed dead,
And there reigns Love and all Love's loving parts,
And all those friends which I thought buried.
How many a holy and obsequious tear
Hath dear religious love stol'n from mine eye,
As interest of the dead, which now appear
But things removed that hidden in thee lie!
Thou art the grave where buried love doth live,
Hung with the trophies of my lovers gone,
Who all their parts of me to thee did give,
That due of many now is thine alone.
  Their images I lov'd I view in thee,
  And thou (all they) hast all the all of me.

YOU ARE THE SHRINE OF LOST LOVES

YOUR BREAST IS made precious by all those hearts which I thought were dead because I had lost them. For love is the king of your heart, and there all of love's loving subjects pay court, including every friend I thought was buried.

Sacred love has exacted from my eyes, like tribute for the dead, many a holy and funereal tear. But now these dead show themselves to be hidden in you, like objects merely moved elsewhere.

You are the memorial where buried love lives on; its adorning trophies are my lost lovers, who give to you all that I gave to them. The affection which many friends once evoked from me is now due to you alone.

I see in yours the faces I have loved. You are all of them. And all the all of me as well belongs to you.

Note: With its multiple alls and parts, this sonnet has echoes of the Dry Bones story in the biblical book of *Ezekiel* (37: 1–14). "One for All, And All for One" was the motto of H.W.'s family. See S8 and S53. / L5: *obsequious*: pertaining to obsequies (funerals).

If thou survive my well-contented day,
When that churl Death my bones with dust
    shall cover,
And shalt by fortune once more re-survey
These poor rude lines of thy deceased lover,
Compare them with the bett'ring of the time,
And though they be outstripped by every pen,
Reserve them for my love, not for their rhyme,
Exceeded by the height of happier men.
O then vouchsafe me but this loving thought:
"Had my friend's Muse grown with this growing
    age,
A dearer birth than this his love had brought
To march in ranks of better equipage:
    But since he died, and poets better prove,
    Theirs for their style I'll read, his for his love."

INFERIOR POEMS, SUPERIOR LOVE

YOU MAY SURVIVE the day when I die, pleased enough to have known your love. Then, when boorish Death has covered my bones with dust, you may by chance reread these poor rude poems from your deceased lover, and compare them with the better ones of later times.

Even if my verses be surpassed by every writer, preserve them for the love that inspired them, if not for the skill which the poetic flights of more favored men will outdo.

May you then grant me this loving consideration: "If my friend's poetic powers had matured into the contemporary style, his love would have produced more precious offspring. These would have taken their place in the ranks of poems written by poets better equipped.

"But since he died unripened, and current poets write better, I'll read their works for style, and his for the love that inspired them."

Note: Though the myriad-mooded W.S. could give his verses immortal value in one sonnet, he could belittle them in the next—if the *Sonnets* are in chronological order. / Ls4, 10: the poet calls himself a lover of the Youth; but in the words which the poet imagines the Youth speaking, he calls himself a friend.

*F*ull many a glorious morning have I seen
  Flatter the mountain tops with sovereign eye,
Kissing with golden face the meadows green,
Gilding pale streams with heavenly alchemy,
Anon permit the basest clouds to ride
With ugly rack on his celestial face,
And from the forlorn world his visage hide,
Stealing unseen to west with this disgrace:
Even so my sun one early morn did shine
With all triumphant splendour on my brow;
But out alack, he was but one hour mine,
The region cloud hath masked him from me now.
  Yet him for this my love no whit disdaineth:
  Suns of the world may stain, when heaven's sun
staineth.

YOU ARE MOODY,
BUT SO IS THE SUN

I HAVE SEEN many a glorious morning beautify
the mountain tops with the royal sun. I've seen that
sun kiss the green meadows with its golden face,
and burnish pale streams with heavenly magic—and
then permit ugly ranks of the lowliest clouds to ride
across its heavenly face, and hide it from forlorn
earthlings as it steals to the west unseen
and shamefully disfigured.

In just that way, one early morning the sun of my
life shone on my face with full triumphant splendor.
But quickly doused, alas, the glory was mine for only
an hour. Local clouds have masked him from me
since then.

Yet for this change, my love faults him not a bit:
if the sun above can be dimmed, so may suns below.

Note: Here is the first evidence of a quarrel between poet and Youth. / L3:
Shakespeare's Sonnets present a rainbow of *color* (4), *hue* (5) or *tincture* (1),
including *black* (13), *white* (7), *green* (5), *red* (4), *yellow* (3), *gold* (2), and one
each of *grey, purple, raven, rosy, sable,* and *vermilion.* But O! Ah! Alas! and
Alack! There is no "blue!" (and only one *sky*)!

34

*Why didst thou promise such a beauteous
day,*

And make me travel forth without my cloak,

To let base clouds o'ertake me in my way,

Hiding thy brav'ry in their rotten smoke?

'Tis not enough that through the cloud thou break,

To dry the rain on my storm-beaten face,

For no man well of such a salve can speak,

That heals the wound and cures not the disgrace:

Nor can thy shame give physic to my grief;

Though thou repent, yet I have still the loss:

The offender's sorrow lends but weak relief

To him that bears the strong offence's cross.

   Ah! but those tears are pearl which thy love sheds,

   And they are rich and ransom all ill deeds.

THE WOUND SURVIVES THE WEAPON

WHY DID YOU promise lovely weather that prompted me to go out without my cloak, and then let ugly clouds overtake me on my way—clouds that hid your splendor in noxious smoke?

It doesn't help when you break through the clouds, and try to dry the rain on my storm-battered face. For who can laud a remedy that eases the immediate damage but doesn't erase the humiliation?

You say that you are ashamed, but my embarrassment remains. The sorrow of the offender is a feeble remedy when the offended person still has to bear the odium of the rough treatment.

Still, the tears which your love sheds are pearls. They are precious, and they atone for all wrongs done.

Note: With its cross-bearing and repentant tears, this sonnet clearly echoes the Passion story of Jesus and the Apostle Peter. Rather riskily, the poet here makes himself a Christ-figure. By way of contrast, Ss 105, 106, 108, 109, 110, and 112 divinize the Fair Youth in various ways.

35

No more be grieved at that which thou
hast done:
Roses have thorns, and silver fountains mud,
Clouds and eclipses stain both moon and sun,
And loathsome canker lives in sweetest bud.
All men make faults, and even I in this,
Authorizing thy trespass with compare,
Myself corrupting, salving thy amiss,
Excusing thy sins more than thy sins are;
For to thy sensual fault I bring in sense—
Thy adverse party is thy advocate—
And 'gainst myself a lawful plea commence:
Such civil war is in my love and hate
That I an accessory needs must be
To that sweet thief which sourly robs from me.

LOVE AND HATE:
WAR WITHIN

DON'T FEEL BAD any longer for what you've done to me. After all, Roses have thorns, and silvery streams their mud; clouds and eclipses mar both moon and sun, and hateful cankers grow in the sweetest buds.

All men commits faults—as I myself am now doing by invoking comparisons to justify your trespasses. Thus I corrupt myself by sterilizing your offense, and by excusing your sins with generosity greater than the sins are.

I bring reason to bear on your unreasoned misbehavior, and so the plaintiff becomes your advocate. I oppose myself by entering a lawyer's plea on your behalf.

My love and my hate are so engulfed in civil war that I force myself to be an accessory to that sweet thief who injures me with his bitter thievings.

Note: L12: this is the only time the poet uses *hate* with reference to his own feelings. Elsewhere he says he is the object of hate from both the Fair Youth (e.g., S89) and the Dark Lady (e.g., S149). / L14: the sweet thieving is perhaps further explained in Ss40–42.

*L*et me confess that we two must be twain,
    Although our undivided loves are one:
So shall those blots that do with me remain,
Without thy help, by me be borne alone.
In our two loves there is but one respect,
Though in our lives a separable spite,
Which though it alter not love's sole effect,
Yet doth it steal sweet hours from love's delight.
I may not evermore acknowledge thee,
Lest my bewailed guilt should do thee shame,
Nor thou with public kindness honour me,
Unless thou take that honour from thy name:
    But do not so; I love thee in such sort,
    As thou being mine, mine is thy good report.

SPLITTING UP FOR YOUR SAKE

LET ME ADMIT IT: we have to split up—even though our mutual love is undivided. That way I'll endure, without your involvement, the bad odor which will cling to me alone.

Your love and mine are in harmony, even though our lives are afflicted by an outside spite that separates us. That spite does not change the single-mindedness of our love, but it does rob that love of sweet hours of delight.

From now on, if my regretted guilt is not to shame you too, I can never openly greet you. For your part, you should not honor me with public favor, for that honor will be deducted from the stature of your name.

No, don't dishonor yourself. My love is such that what is yours is mine. Therefore your decent reputation is mine as well.

Note: The damaging scandal is unidentified. It isn't clear whether the accusations are entirely justified (*my bewailed guilt*), or at least partly due to the *spite* of third parties. / Curiously, the final two lines will also end S96, where they are not as good a fit.

*As a decrepit father takes delight
To see his active child do deeds of youth,
So I, made lame by Fortune's dearest spite,
Take all my comfort of thy worth and truth;
For whether beauty, birth, or wealth, or wit,
Or any of these all, or all, or more,
Entitled in thy parts do crowned sit,
I make my love engrafted to this store:
So then I am not lame, poor, nor despised,
Whilst that this shadow doth such substance give,
That I in thy abundance am sufficed,
And by a part of all thy glory live.
  Look what is best, that best I wish in thee:
  This wish I have; then ten times happy me.*

YOUR YOUTH RESTORES MY LOST YOUTH

A BROKEN-DOWN FATHER rejoices to see his energetic youngster busy with youthful deeds. So I, crippled by the worst that fate can inflict, take all my comfort in your outer and inner excellence.

I graft my affections onto your abundance—to some, or all, or more than all of your handsomeness, ancestry, wealth, and wit, indeed to whatever riches rightly crown your multi-layered self.

Thus it happens that I am not lame or poor or despised so long as even your shadow imparts substance to me. That is abundance enough to answer all my needs. I exist, thanks to even a fragment of your glory.

Imagine the best of good fortunes. That is what I wish for you. If my wish is granted, my happiness will be tenfold.

Note: A poet compares and contrasts. The *Sonnets* speak of *good* (15), *better* (19), and *best* (22). *More* is one of the most frequent sonnet words (64); *most* has 27 hits, *much*, 18; *part*, 20; *full*, 2; *great*, 10; *large*, 5; two each for *small*, *little*, and *huge*; one each for *big*, *tall*, *stout*, and *thin*. The *Sonnets* are, however, "fat" free.

38

How can my Muse want subject to invent
  While thou dost breathe, that pour'st into
    my verse
Thine own sweet argument, too excellent
For every vulgar paper to rehearse?
O give thyself the thanks if aught in me
Worthy perusal stand against thy sight,
For who's so dumb that cannot write to thee,
When thou thyself dost give invention light?
Be thou the tenth Muse, ten times more in worth
Than those old nine which rhymers invocate,
And he that calls on thee, let him bring forth
Eternal numbers to outlive long date.
    If my slight Muse do please these curious days,
    The pain be mine, but thine shall be the praise.

WHAT VERSIFIER WOULD YOU NOT INSPIRE?

AS LONG AS you are alive, how can my poetic Muse lack creative inspiration? Into the mold of my verses you pour your sweet self as a theme—a theme too elevated for any old scribbler to tackle.

Give yourself credit if your eyes encounter any writing of mine worth reading. Is there anyone so mute that he couldn't write about you, when you yourself shed light on creativity?

You are the Tenth Muse, ten times more potent than those ancient Nine whom rhymers invoke. Let the poet who calls on you produce eternal verses to outlive a great length of years.

If my slight offerings please today's finicky readers, let the painful effort be mine, but yours the applause.

Note: This sonnet raises a question about the speaker's Muse: does she operate inside the poet (*my slight Muse*) or within the inspiring loved one (*be thou the tenth Muse*)? / L13: The poet here implies that the Youth is not the only reader of these *Sonnets*. The earliest (1598) reference to Shakespearean sonnets speaks of them as circulating "among his private friends."

39

O *how thy worth with manners may I sing,*
    When thou art all the better part of me?
What can mine own praise to mine own self bring?
And what is't but mine own when I praise thee?
Even for this, let us divided live,
And our dear love lose name of single one,
That by this separation I may give
That due to thee which thou deserv'st alone.
O absence! what a torment wouldst thou prove,
Were it not thy sour leisure gave sweet leave
To entertain the time with thoughts of love,
Which time and thoughts so sweetly doth deceive,
    And that thou teachest how to make one twain,
    By praising him here who doth hence remain.

HOW CAN I PRAISE YOU WITHOUT SELF-PRAISE?

HOW CAN I SING your praises with modesty, when you are the better half of me? What value has the honor which a man bestows on himself? Yet that's exactly what I'm doing when I praise you.

Here then is another reason why we should live apart, and make our dear love seem two instead of one. Separated from you, I can give you the honor due to yourself alone.

O Absence! You would be sheer torture if your bitter leisure did not provide a sweet occasion for me to ransom the time with thoughts of love, love which sweetly beguiles both time and thought.

Yes, sour Absence, you teach me also how to treat a single love as double, since I am here, modestly praising someone who isn't here.

Note: This sonnet enjoys the rarity of having two addressees: the real Youth and abstract Absence. / As the next 3 sonnets will make clear, the poet had a mistress, with whom the dear Youth had been betrayingly intimate. Many scholars think she is the "Dark Lady" of the final 28 poems (Ss127–154), and that the episode of Ss40–42 is the same one which is implied in S35, and preoccupies Ss133–144.

40

Take all my loves, my love, yea, take them all;
 What hast thou then more than thou hadst
  before?
No love, my love, that thou mayst true love call;
All mine was thine, before thou hadst this more.
Then if for my love thou my love receivest,
I cannot blame thee for my love thou usest;
But yet be blamed, if thou thyself deceivest
By wilful taste of what thyself refusest.
I do forgive thy robb'ry, gentle thief,
Although thou steal thee all my poverty;
And yet love knows it is a greater grief
To bear love's wrong than hate's known injury.
 Lascivious grace, in whom all ill well shows,
 Kill me with spites; yet we must not be foes.

YOU HAVE EVERYTHING ELSE: TAKE MY SPECIAL ONE

ALL RIGHT, BELOVED ONE, take for yourself absolutely everything I love. What would you have then that you don't already have? Certainly no love that you could call true love.

Everything I had was yours before you made your latest conquest. If you steal what I love because I was already the conqueror, then I can't blame you if, for the same reason, you enjoy what you take.

But I will blame you if you are deceiving yourself into the forced enjoyment of what you otherwise would not have chosen.

I pardon your robbery, gentle thief, even though you steal all of the little I have. Yet anyone who has ever loved realizes that there is keener hurt in love betrayed than in the injuries which hatred deliberately inflicts.

Lust-lovely lover, in you every illness looks like health. Slay me with abuse; but we mustn't turn into enemies.

Note: Most readers presume that this sonnet refers to a woman. But why? How cleverly it skirts the issue of gender! But again, why? The next two poems in this triad will clarify the matter. / L13: in various forms, *grace* makes 19 appearances in *Shakespeare's Sonnets*.

41

*T*hose pretty wrongs that liberty commits,
    When I am sometime absent from thy heart,
Thy beauty and thy years full well befits,
For still temptation follows where thou art.
Gentle thou art, and therefore to be won,
Beauteous thou art, therefore to be assailed;
And when a woman woos, what woman's son
Will sourly leave her till she have prevailed?
Ay me! but yet thou might'st my seat forbear,
And chide thy beauty and thy straying youth,
Who lead thee in their riot even there
Where thou art forced to break a twofold truth:
    Hers, by thy beauty tempting her to thee,
    Thine, by thy beauty being false to me.

PRETTY SINS,
UGLY SCHISMS

YOU ARE FREE to commit your pretty sins when
I at times am absent from your heart. And so you do,
for such sins come with your beauty and with your
young years, when temptation stalks you constantly.

Highborn, you are a trophy to be won. Handsome,
you are a fortress to be assailed. And when a woman
comes a-wooing, what woman's son will discourteously
abandon her before she triumphs?

Still, you might have stayed away from my pasture,
or else, repenting, speedily chastized your beauty
and your deviating youth.

For in their intensity both beauty and youth have
propelled you into a situation where your charms forced
the breaking of two commitments: hers to me, by
tempting her away; yours to me, by playing me false.

Note: L1: in the *Sonnets* there is only one other *pretty* (S132). / L4: *still* often
means "constantly." / L10: temptation first follows, then leads. The following
may have been done by the Youth's hangers-on and other companions. / The
next sonnet will use three of the 19 *friends*, already introduced in S29. The
only *foe* is in S1; there are also *wars* (7), *enemies* (2), and *peace* (2). There is
no "truce."

*T*hat thou hast her, it is not all my grief,
  And yet it may be said I loved her dearly;
That she hath thee is of my wailing chief,
A loss in love that touches me more nearly.
Loving offenders, thus I will excuse ye:
Thou dost love her because thou know'st I love her,
And for my sake even so doth she abuse me,
Suff'ring my friend for my sake to approve her.
If I lose thee, my loss is my love's gain,
And losing her, my friend hath found that loss;
Both find each other, and I lose both twain,
And both for my sake lay on me this cross.
    But here's the joy; my friend and I are one;
    Sweet flattery! then she loves but me alone.

FINDING SOLACE IN A DOUBLE BETRAYAL

MY PRESENT PAIN doesn't entirely derive from the fact that you have stolen my mistress—though you could say I loved her dearly. That she now possesses you is my main grief, for that is a love-loss that cuts closer to the nerve.

Still, I will invent excuses for both you loving offenders: 1) you love her because you know that I love her; and 2) for my sake too she betrays me, since it is a friend of mine she permits to win her favor.

If I lose you to her, my friend, someone I love will gain in the process. If I lose her to you, a friend will have found what I lost. Friend and sweetheart find each other; I lose both, yet it is for my sake that they crucify me.

I find some joy in the fact that my friend and I are one. For I indulge in the sweet flattery of rationalizing that it is actually only me whom she is loving.

Note: L8: unexpectedly, the *Sonnets* have no other *suffering*, though in addition to *suffer* (3), they have five related ideas: *grief* (7), *wounds* (4), *torment* and *torture* (2 each), and one *hurt* (but no "ache" or "agony"). / In mid-poem the Youth stops being a *thou*, and becomes someone talked about. This sonnet concludes for now a series of betrayal poems.

43

When most I wink, then do mine eyes best see,

For all the day they view things unrespected;
But when I sleep, in dreams they look on thee,
And darkly bright, are bright in dark directed.
Then thou, whose shadow shadows doth make bright,
How would thy shadow's form form happy show
To the clear day with thy much clearer light,
When to unseeing eyes thy shade shines so!
How would (I say) mine eyes be blessed made
By looking on thee in the living day,
When in dead night thy fair imperfect shade
Through heavy sleep on sightless eyes doth stay!

All days are nights to see till I see thee,

And nights bright days when dreams do show
thee me.

I'LL SEE YOU IN MY DREAMS

—GUS CAHN

MY EYES SEE most clearly when I am most asleep.
For all the day long I look at things I don't care
about. But when I slumber, I see you in my dreams,
dreams which are bright in their darkness from a
brightness shining on the dark itself.

During the day, back home, your very shadow
normally brightens up the shadows! Now, away from
you, how the night's shade gleams luminously in
my shut eyes! How much more, then, would your
form create a happy sight if it could be viewed more
clearly in the clarity of day.

I mean, since in the dead of night and through
thick sleep your lovely but unreal shape beams
steadily on my unseeing eyes, how much more would
these eyes of mine be blessed if they could gaze on
you by living sunlight!

All days will seem but nights until I see you, but
nights turn into sunny days when you show up in
my dreams.

Note: Almost humorously, this sonnet makes the same point repeatedly. /
L14: *show thee [to] me* would be clearer than *show thee me.* The oddness
may have stemmed from the poet's need to rhyme the final word with *thee.*

If the dull substance of my flesh were thought,
Injurious distance should not stop my way,
For then despite of space I would be brought,
From limits far remote, where thou dost stay.
No matter then although my foot did stand
Upon the farthest earth removed from thee,
For nimble thought can jump both sea and land
As soon as think the place where he would be.
But ah, thought kills me that I am not thought,
To leap large lengths of miles when thou art gone,
But that, so much of earth and water wrought,
I must attend time's leisure with my moan,

Receiving nought by elements so slow
But heavy tears, badges of either's woe.

LONGING FOR THE SPEED OF THOUGHT

IF MY SLUGGISH BODY were pure thought, hurtful distances could never block my path. For then, however remote you were, I would speed to your side from the farthest remove. It wouldn't matter then even if my feet were planted on the spot of earth most distant from you.

For nimble thought can leap over land and sea as swiftly as it can think of the beloved's location. Ah! the thought that I am not thought quite slays me. For when you are away, I cannot come bounding over these many miles between us.

But since I am composed of earth and water, I must grievingly endure the slowness of time. From elements so retarding I gain nothing but heavy tears, the emblems of our mutual sorrow.

Note: In this sonnet and the next, the poet refers to what were once regarded as the four basic ingredients of all material reality: earth, air, fire, and water. Here he focuses on earth/flesh and water/tears.

45

*T*he other two [elements], slight air and
    purging fire,
Are both with thee, wherever I abide;
The first my thought, the other my desire,
These present–absent with swift motion slide.
For when these quicker elements are gone
In tender embassy of love to thee,
My life, being made of four, with two alone
Sinks down to death, oppressed with melancholy,
Until life's composition be recured
By those swift messengers returned from thee,
Who even but now come back again, assured
Of thy fair health, recounting it to me.
    This told, I joy; but then no longer glad,
    I send them back again, and straight grow sad.

LOVE LETTERS STRAIGHT FROM THE HEART

—Victor Young

OF THE QUARTET of basic elements, thin air and purifying fire remain with you no matter where I am. Air is my thought; fire is my desire. They are present with us even in our absence. Neither dull nor heavy, these two elements move swiftly. But when they wing off to you as ambassadors of my tender love, my body, composed of all four elements, sinks down death-ward, heavy with sadness from the remaining earth and water.

Such is my condition until my nature is restored by the return of my fleet-footed messengers. This happened just now, and they have reassured me by detailing your good health.

I rejoice to hear the upbeat news. But then, as the substitute gladness fades, I send the messengers off to you once more, and slump back again into instant sadness.

Note: Focusing now on air and fire, this sonnet continues the previous one. Possibly thinking of love letters between him and his beloved, the poet imagines the messages in them as being composed of the air of thought and the fire of desire.

46

Mine eye and heart are at a mortal war,
How to divide the conquest of thy sight:
Mine eye my heart thy picture's sight would bar,
My heart mine eye the freedom of that right.
My heart doth plead that thou in him dost lie
(A closet never pierced with crystal eyes),
But the defendant doth that plea deny
And says in him thy fair appearance lies.
To 'cide this title is impannelled
A quest of thoughts, all tenants to the heart,
And by their verdict is determined
The clear eye's moiety and the dear heart's part,
  As thus; mine eye's due is thy outward part,
  And my heart's right thy inward love of heart.

A BATTLE AND BALLOT

MY EYE AND MY HEART are in a kind of deadly battle over how to divide the spoils of your appearance. My eye wants to block my heart from claiming you. My heart wants to deny my eye the right to do the same.

My heart argues that your true visage is locked within it—a hideaway never pierced by outward eyes. But the defending eye denies that argument, and claims that it sees your true image.

To decide the case, an inquest of thoughts (each one a tenant of the heart) has been summoned to court. Their verdict will determine what belongs to the clear eye, and what to the endeared heart.

And the verdict is this: my eye's portion is your external appearance; to my heart belongs your heart's inward love.

Note: The mini-drama of this sonnet is rather undramatic. / L10: the eye has pictures, but the heart has thoughts. So a thinking jury would be expected to be partial to the heart. The conflict between seeing and feeling, appearance and reality, heart and head is ancient and ongoing, and central to the *Sonnets*: "Tell me where is fancy bred,/Or in the heart or in the head?" (*The Merchant of Venice* 3.2.65).

47

Betwixt mine eye and heart a league is took,
And each doth good turns now unto the
   other:
When that mine eye is famished for a look,
Or heart in love with sighs himself doth smother,
With my love's picture then my eye doth feast
And to the painted banquet bids my heart;
Another time mine eye is my heart's guest,
And in his thoughts of love doth share a part.
So either by thy picture or my love,
Thyself, away, art present still with me,
For thou not farther than my thoughts canst move,
And I am still with them, and they with thee;
   Or, if they sleep, thy picture in my sight
   Awakes my heart to heart's and eye's delight.

A MUTUAL ASSISTANCE TREATY

MY EYE AND MY HEART have signed a treaty, and now they take turns helping each other. When my eye is famished for a glance at you, or my heart is smothering itself with sighs of separation, my eye feasts on your picture and invites my heart to the painted banquet.

At other times my eye is my heart's guest, and shares in its loving thoughts. So, either by outward picture or inward love, you are present to me when you are away. For you can't go farther than my thoughts can, and I am always with them, and they with you.

Or if my thoughts are slumbering, your image dreams itself into view and awakens my heart to one who delights both heart and eye.

Note: Only two likenesses of W.S., both posthumous, are surely authentic: 1) the frontispiece of the *First Folio* (1623), a copper engraving by Martin Droeshout. Only 15 when W.S. died, he probably worked from someone's earlier portrait, now lost; 2) Gheerart Janssen's soft stone bust near W.S.'s grave. His shop was near the Bard's Globe theatre. Kin and friends presumably saw and approved both images. The right hand of W.S.'s bust gets a new quill each year on his April 23rd birthday. The popular and romantic "Chandos" painting (with its left earring) may have been painted from life by the great actor Richard Burbage.

How careful was I, when I took my way,
    Each trifle under truest bars to thrust,
That to my use it might unused stay
From hands of falsehood, in sure wards of trust!
But thou, to whom my jewels trifles are,
Most worthy comfort, now my greatest grief,
Thou best of dearest, and mine only care,
Art left the prey of every vulgar thief.
Thee have I not locked up in any chest,
Save where thou art not, though I feel thou art,
Within the gentle closure of my breast,
From whence at pleasure thou mayst come and part;
    And even thence thou wilt be stol'n, I fear,
    For truth proves thievish for a prize so dear.

WILL YOU BE STOLEN FROM MY HEART?

WHENEVER I WENT on a trip, I was always extremely careful to stuff each trifling treasure of mine under the sturdiest locks. That way, as though guarded by a trusty warden, each valuable stayed safe from alien hands and reserved for my exclusive enjoyment.

But such treasures are mere trifles compared to you—you who were once my chief source of comfort but who are now my greatest grief. You are the best of my dearest and my sole concern. But now you are the prey of every common thief.

I never locked you up in any kind of treasure chest, except within the tender confines of my heart. You are not there now, though I still feel your presence there. You have always been free to come and go as you wish.

But I'm afraid you'll be stolen even from there. For honesty itself will turn thievish for such a prize.

Note: This is the only sonnet which uses the word *trifle*. To modern lovers of W.S.'s plays, it is jolting to see them thrice referred to as "trifles" in the dedication of the historic *First Folio* (1623). This word, chosen by the twin editors (his friends and fellow actors), reflects the low esteem in which plays were held at that time by the upper class, to two of whom the *Folio* was dedicated.

A gainst that time, if ever that time come,
When I shall see thee frown on my defects,
When as thy love hath cast his utmost sum,
Called to that audit by advised respects;
Against that time when thou shalt strangely pass
And scarcely greet me with that sun, thine eye,
When love converted from the thing it was
Shall reasons find of settled gravity:
Against that time do I ensconce me here
Within the knowledge of mine own desert,
And this my hand against myself uprear,
To guard the lawful reasons on thy part.

    To leave poor me thou hast the strength of laws,
    Since why to love I can allege no cause.

IF EVER YOU SHOULD LEAVE ME

THE TIME MAY COME when I shall see you frowning on my faults, and, as a result of a reasonable audit, your love for me will have spent its last penny.

The time may come when you will walk past me like a stranger, scarcely greeting me with the sunshine of your eyes.

The time may come when your love for me will find serious grounds for having changed from what it used to be.

With that possibility in mind, I take the stand in the court of my own self-knowledge, and raise my hand against myself to justify your legitimate complaints.

It will be lawful and sensible for you to leave a friend who has so little to offer, since I can't think of any reason why you should love me.

Note: Here it is only the Fair Youth's love which is envisioned as changing. In S116 the poet will insist that "love is not love/Which alters when it alteration finds." Here and elsewhere in the *Sonnets*, the poet's self-humiliation and lack of self-esteem are painful to behold.

50

How heavy do I journey on the way,
When what I seek, my weary travel's end,
Doth teach that ease and that repose to say,
"Thus far the miles are measured from thy friend."
The beast that bears me, tired with my woe,
Plods dully on, to bear that weight in me,
As if by some instinct the wretch did know
His rider loved not speed, being made from thee:
The bloody spur cannot provoke him on
That sometimes anger thrusts into his hide,
Which heavily he answers with a groan
More sharp to me than spurring to his side;

For that same groan doth put this in my mind:
My grief lies onward, and my joy behind.

PALE HORSE, PALE RIDER

—KATHERINE ANNE PORTER

HOW HEAVILY DO I journey on, when the goal
I seek—the day's end of my weary traveling—will
merely give me the comfort and the relaxation to
say, "These many more miles have I traveled from
my friend!"

The horse that carries me, tired with my fatigue
and heavy with my heaviness, plods on listlessly, as if
by some instinct the nag knew that its rider had no
love for any speed that takes me away from you. The
bloody spur which I sometimes angrily thrust into
its side cannot make it trot any faster. He answers
my thrust with a heavy groan that is sharper to me
than a spur in its side.

For that same groan renews the thought that
grief lies ahead of me, and joy behind.

Note: The 73-mile journey between London and W.S.'s family at Stratford could
take 3 days on horseback. In Oxford, 50 miles west of the capital, tourists can
see a room in a former inn where the poet is said to have often stayed. Sir
William Davenant (1606–1668), English poet laureate and putative son of the
innkeeper, claimed to be the Bard's love child and godson. / L5: the *Sonnets*
provide us with *beasts* and *horses* (2 apiece), one *herd*, *jade*, *lamb*, *lion*, *tiger*,
and *wolf*; also, *worms* and *birds* (4 apiece), *crows* (2), along with one *dove*, *lark*,
phoenix, and *feathered creature*. There is no "animal."

51

Thus can my love excuse the slow offence
Of my dull bearer when from thee I speed:
From where thou art, why should I haste me thence?
Till I return, of posting is no need.
O, what excuse will my poor beast then find,
When swift extremity can seem but slow?
Then should I spur though mounted on the wind,
In winged speed no motion shall I know:
Then can no horse with my desire keep pace;
Therefore desire, of perfect'st love being made,
Shall neigh, no dull flesh, in his fiery race,
But love, for love, thus shall excuse my jade:
   Since from thee going he went wilful-slow,
   Towards thee I'll run, and give him leave to go.

MY DULL HORSE:
GOING AND COMING

WHY SHOULD I depart quickly when it's you I'm leaving? That's the excuse my amorous heart uses to forgive the sluggish horse who takes me away from you. There will be no need for speed until I'm on my way back.

What excuse will my poor beast have then, when the fastest speed would seem slow? Even if I were riding the wind I would still use my spurs. The wings of speed [on Pegasus] will scarcely seem to move at all. For there's no horse that could keep pace then with my eagerness.

This impetuosity of mine derives from the most perfect love. In its fiery racing, my passion will be no lifeless neighing mount. Out of the generosity of love, my love will still excuse this nag: since his slow motion was deliberate when he was leaving you, I'll hasten to you in spirit and let him plod along at his own pace without me.

Note: L4: *posting*: use of a commercial speed horse between posts (travel stations). Such a horse could cover as much as 100 miles a day, more than three times faster than a regular horse. / L8: the mythical winged horse Pegasus may be intended here. / In the next sonnet those seldom coming feast days of Ls 5–6 recall the playing holidays which, "when they seldom come, they wish'd for come" (*Henry IV*, Part I, 1.2.181).

So am I as the rich whose blessed key
Can bring him to his sweet up-locked treasure,
The which he will not ev'ry hour survey,
For blunting the fine point of seldom pleasure.
Therefore are feasts so solemn and so rare,
Since, seldom coming, in the long year set,
Like stones of worth they thinly placed are,
Or captain jewels in the carcanet.
So is the time that keeps you as my chest,
Or as the wardrobe which the robe doth hide,
To make some special instant special blest,
By new unfolding his imprison'd pride.
*   Blessed are you, whose worthiness gives scope,*
*   Being had, to triumph; being lacked, to hope.*

THE FINE POINT OF SELDOM PLEASURES

I AM LIKE A RICH MAN with a key that gives him blessed access to his sweet, locked-up treasure. But he doesn't use the key every hour to survey his wealth. If he did, he would "blunt the fine point of seldom pleasure."

That's why feast days are both solemn and rare: seldom coming, they are spaced out thinly like precious stones set in the long year, or like the chief jewels of a necklace.

Your time away from me is like that treasure chest, or like the wardrobe that hides a lovely robe: that time of absence will make some special moment especially blissful by revealing anew the splendor imprisoned within your absence.

You are a blessing because your excellence causes joy when you are present, and hope when you are absent.

Note: W.S. may have been paid from 6 to 10 pounds for writing and producing a play. Since there were no banks, he invested. Such comparisons are shaky, but a pound may have been worth about $45 in 1600. Guesses at his variable annual income range from 50 to 100 pounds. The average middle class laborer's income has been estimated as 20 pounds. At his death his cash estate was some 350 pounds. He left a hefty 10 pounds for the poor, but nothing for the preacher. A trustee of the church, W.S. was buried in its sanctuary.

53

*W*hat is your substance, whereof are you
made,

That millions of strange shadows on you tend?

Since every one hath, every one, one shade,

And you, but one, can every shadow lend.

Describe Adonis, *and the counterfeit*

Is poorly imitated after you;

On Helen's *cheek all art of beauty set,*

And you in Grecian *tires are painted new:*

Speak of the spring and foison of the year:

The one doth shadow of your beauty show,

The other as your bounty doth appear,

And you in every blessed shape we know.

> *In all external grace you have some part,*
>
> *But you like none, none you, for constant heart.*

MILLIONS OF
SHADOWS STRANGE

THERE ARE SUCH countless and exotic aspects to your personality that I have to ask, which is your essential self, of what stuff are you made? Most people have a single self; but you can exhibit every variety of self, though you yourself are one.

Let someone describe Adonis: the depiction will be a pale imitation of you. Let someone apply all the arts of beauty to Helen's cheek, and then he'll have a painting of you in Grecian attire.

Picture the spring or the autumn of the year: the one season shows merely the shadow of your beauty; the other bespeaks your mellow fruitfulness. Indeed, you appear in every blessed form that's known.

Yes, you have some part in every outward grace there is. But in the constancy of your heart, you are like none, and none is like you.

Note: See S101 for Plato's handling of the problem of the One and the Many. / *Shakespeare's Sonnets* contain few mythical references. The poet, however, had already dedicated his *Venus and Adonis* (both cited here) to the Earl of Southampton (H.W.), who may be the Youth of these poems. / On W.S.'s stage, boys played the parts of women like Helen. In view of earlier accusations, the last line seems quite excessive, like the *millions* of L2.

O *how much more doth beauty beauteous seem*
 By that sweet ornament which truth doth
   give!
The Rose looks fair, but fairer we it deem
For that sweet odour which doth in it live.
The canker blooms have full as deep a dye
As the perfumed tincture of the Roses,
Hang on such thorns, and play as wantonly,
When summer's breath their masked buds discloses:
But, for their virtue only is their show,
They live unwooed and unrespected fade,
Die to themselves. Sweet Roses do not so,
Of their sweet deaths are sweetest odours made:
   And so of you, beauteous and lovely youth,
   When that shall fade, my verse distils your truth.

PRESERVING YOUR BETTER BEAUTY

BEAUTY SEEMS so much more beautiful when true inner loveliness enhances it. The Rose looks outwardly winsome, but we deem it lovelier for the sweet odor residing within.

Wild poppies are dyed as deeply as the perfumed color of roses. They too hang on thorns and sway as freely when the breath of summer unmasks their buds.

But since their only virtue is their show, they live unsought and fade unnoticed, dying to themselves alone.

Such is not the case with sweet roses: from their deaths come most delicious fragrances.

It's the same with you, beautiful Youth, gracious Youth. When your youth fades, my poems will preserve its essence.

Note: Though entitled *Shakespeare's Sonnets*, the sonnets themselves never use the word "sonnet," or even "poem" or "poetry" (but *poesy* once). Instead, the poet uses many synonyms: *verses* (16), *words* (12), *lines* and *pen* (10), *rhymes* (6), *singing* and *book* (7), *songs* (5), *numbers* (4), *lays* (3), *pages* (1), *papers* (1), *pencil* (1), and *ink* (2). He uses *poet* six times, refers to himself as one, and twice imagines himself being called one. / L5: it isn't clear which flower (*canker blooms*) the poet is here contrasting with the *Rose*, thrice mentioned.

55

Not marble nor the gilded monuments
Of princes shall outlive this pow'rful rhyme,
But you shall shine more bright in these contents
Than unswept stone, besmeared with sluttish time.
When wasteful war shall Statues overturn,
And broils root out the work of masonry,
Nor Mars his sword nor war's quick fire shall burn
The living record of your memory.
'Gainst death and all-oblivious enmity
Shall you pace forth; your praise shall still find room
Even in the eyes of all posterity
That wear this world out to the ending doom.
    So, till the Judgement that yourself arise,
    You live in this, and dwell in lovers' eyes.

GOLDEN WORDS: THE STURDIEST STATUES

NEITHER MARBLE NOR the gilded monuments of princes will outlive these mighty sonnets. Within them you will shine more brightly than any stone plaque that lies unswept, and smudged with time's filthy fingers.

Let wasteful war overturn statues. Let conflicts shatter the grandest masonry. Neither the wrath of the war god Mars nor his sudden fires will consume this living record of your memory.

In the face of death and of the hatred that destroys remembrance, you will march bravely onward. Your praise will ever find its place in the eyes of all posterity as they wear out the world till doomsday.

Thus, until you rise again on Judgment Day, you will keep on breathing in this book, and find your home in the eyes of lovers.

Note: L7: *Mars,* another rare mythic reference. / This idea of immortality conferred by poetry goes back at least to the pre-Christian Roman writer Horace (65–8 B.C.E.): "I have built a monument more lasting than bronze." In his case, though, it was himself who was to be immortalized by his poetry. See S107 for a rare hint of this expectation in W.S.

56

Sweet love, renew thy force; be it not said
Thy edge should blunter be than appetite,
Which but today by feeding is allayed,
Tomorrow sharpen'd in his former might:
So, love, be thou; although today thou fill
Thy hungry eyes even till they wink with fullness,
Tomorrow see again, and do not kill
The spirit of love with a perpetual dullness.
Let this sad Interim like the ocean be
Which parts the shore, where two contracted new
Come daily to the banks, that, when they see
Return of love, more blest may be the view;

    Else call it winter, which being full of care
    Makes summer's welcome thrice more wished,
more rare.

ABSENCE, MAKE THE HEART GROW!

SWEET LOVE THAT dwells within me, renew your vigor! Let it not be said that your edge is duller than that of bodily appetites. By being fed, these hungers are quieted today, but tomorrow will be as keen as ever.

So, love, you be that way too. Even though today you indulge your hungry eyes so much that they droop from abundance, tomorrow let them open wide again. Otherwise you will kill the spirit of love with a chronic dullness.

Ours is a sad period of separation. Let it be like an ocean that parts the shores where lovers newly engaged come alone to either edge day by day. Thus, when they finally see love returning, their eyes will feel even more blessed than they did before.

Or call this time winter, full of frosty cares, which makes the return of summer three times more yearned for, thrice as precious.

Note: L1: the *sweet love* could be the poet's or his friend's. / L11: since an ocean does the separating, the returning love must involve a looked-for ship.

57

*B*eing your slave, what should I do but tend
  Upon the hours and times of your desire?
I have no precious time at all to spend,
Nor services to do, till you require.
Nor dare I chide the world-without-end hour
Whilst I, my sovereign, watch the clock for you,
Nor think the bitterness of absence sour
When you have bid your servant once adieu.
Nor dare I question with my jealous thought
Where you may be, or your affairs suppose,
But, like a sad slave, stay and think of nought
Save, where you are, how happy you make those.
    So true a fool is love that in your will,
    Though you do anything, he thinks no ill.

WAITING ON YOU
AND FOR YOU

SINCE I AM YOUR SLAVE, what duty do I have but to wait upon the hours and the times of your wishes? My time is not precious nor have I anything to do until you require some service.

I wouldn't dare grumble about the endless minutes I spend watching the clock for your royal arrival. Nor would I regard as sour the bitterness of absence when once you have bid me goodbye. I wouldn't dare let my jealous thoughts question where you might be, or imagine what you might be doing.

No, like a downcast slave I stay put and think of nothing but of how happy you are making others, wherever you are. My love is such a faithful fool that it would find no fault in anything you did.

Note: In this ironic sonnet, the resentful poet reveals that he is doing the very things he says he dare not do as a slave, a servant, a fool. / L13: is *your will* Shakespeare? (For this *will* see also Ss 58, 80, 89, 135, 136, and 143.) By way of the French *Guillaume*, William derives from the Germanic *Wil/helm*, i.e., willing to be a helmet=ready to protect=a defender. The most popular boy's name in W.S.'s day, it was not even a biblical name! It fit W.S.'s last name well, making him "a defender ready to shake a speare." The given name adorned other star poets: Blake, Wordsworth, Yeats.

58

That god forbid that made me first your slave,
I should in thought control your times of
  pleasure,
Or at your hand th'account of hours to crave,
Being your vassal, bound to stay your leisure!
O! let me suffer, being at your beck,
The imprison'd absence of your liberty;
And patience, tame to sufferance, bide each check,
Without accusing you of injury.
Be where you list, your charter is so strong
That you yourself may privilege your time
To what you will; to you it doth belong
Yourself to pardon of self-doing crime.
  I am to wait, though waiting so be hell,
  Not blame your pleasure, be it ill or well.

THE HELL OF WAITING

MAY THE LOVE GOD, who enslaved me to you in
the first place, keep even my thoughts from wanting
to control your pleasurable moments, or from
yearning for an account of how you spend your time.
For I am your vassal, bound to wait at your leisure.

Since I am at your beck and call, let me suffer
the imprisonment of absence which you are free
to impose. Let me learn the patience required by
humble acceptance. Let me endure each of your
rebuffs without accusing you of injury.

Be where you want to be. Your charter of
freedom is so broad that you have the privilege of
using your time as you wish. It is your prerogative to
pardon yourself for any wrongdoing.

My role is to wait, even though such waiting
be hell. It is not my role to blame your pleasure-
seeking, whether it does harm or good.

Note: As in S57, using the principle of "rich indirection," the poet affirms by
denying. The final rhymes of S57, *will* and *ill* have here become *well* and *hell.*

59

If there be nothing new, but that which is
Hath been before, how are our brains beguil'd,
Which, labouring for invention, bear amiss
The second burden of a former child!
O, that record could with a backward look,
Even of five hundred courses of the sun,
Show me your image in some antique book,
Since mind at first in character was done,
That I might see what the old world could say
To this composed wonder of your frame;
Whether we are mended, or where better they,
Or whether revolution be the same.
   O sure I am, the wits of former days
   To subjects worse have given admiring praise.

ARE YOU TRULY
SOMETHING NEW?

IF THERE REALLY IS nothing new under the sun, but all that exists has existed before, how our brains are deceived when, laboring to be inventive, they unknowingly give a second birth to a former child!

Would that I could thumb through records stretching back half a thousand years and find you described in some antique book, composed when thoughts could first be written down.

Then might I see what the old world could say about the wonder of your harmonious presence. Have we improved on the art of description, or was older better? Or has the spinning of the sun made no difference?

At least I'm sure of this: the poets of former times have given admiring praise to persons less worthy.

Note: L1: "There is nothing new under the sun" (*Ecclesiastes* 1:9). / L6: why 500 years? An ancient idea held that every half millennium all cosmic elements return to their original position. Also, the legendary Phoenix had a 500-year cycle. / This sonnet anticipates in several ways Ss 106 and 123.

60

*L*ike as the waves make towards the pebbled
    shore,

So do our minutes hasten to their end,

Each changing place with that which goes before,

In sequent toil all forwards do contend.

Nativity, once in the main of light,

Crawls to maturity, wherewith being crown'd,

Crooked eclipses 'gainst his glory fight,

And Time that gave doth now his gift confound.

Time doth transfix the flourish set on youth

And delves the parallels in beauty's brow,

Feeds on the rarities of nature's truth,

And nothing stands but for his scythe to mow.

    And yet to times in hope my verse shall stand,

    Praising thy worth, despite his cruel hand.

TIME MARCHES ON; SO MAY THESE POEMS

LIKE WAVES WASHING their way toward the pebbled beach, so do our minutes hasten to their end. Each moment takes the place of its predecessor, and all of them struggle in turn to push ahead.

Bathed at first in the full brightness of being, the newborn child crawls on to maturity. Crowned by that maturity, life then finds its glory under attack by malignant shadows.

For at this point Time negates its own gifts. It scars the lovely lines of youth, then etches defacing parallels in beauty's brow. Time feeds on even the truest marvels of nature, for nothing rises up but its scythe will mow it down.

Still, this is my hope: withstanding Time's brutal blows, my sonnets in praise of you will stand tall through ages to come.

Note: S60 talks about *our minutes*, and, of course, 60 minutes make our hour. Recall the 12 hours of the clock in S12.

61

*I*s it thy will thy image should keep open
   My heavy eyelids to the weary night?
Dost thou desire my slumbers should be broken,
While shadows like to thee do mock my sight?
Is it thy spirit that thou send'st from thee
So far from home into my deeds to pry,
To find out shames and idle hours in me,
The scope and tenure of thy jealousy?
O no! thy love, though much, is not so great:
It is my love that keeps mine eye awake;
Mine own true love that doth my rest defeat,
To play the watchman ever for thy sake.

   For thee watch I, whilst thou dost wake elsewhere,

   From me far off, with others all too near.

MY SLEEPLESS NIGHTS
ARE NOT YOUR FAULT

IS THIS WHAT you want?—that your image should keep my heavy eyelids open throughout the weary night? Is it your desire that my slumber be broken by teasing shadows that look like you?

Do you send your ghost all the long way from home to pry into my deeds, my shames, my idleness? Is that the point of some jealousy of yours?

O, no! Though your love is large, it doesn't care that much! It is my love for you that keeps my eyes awake. It is my own true love that defeats my resting hours, as I ever play the watchman for your sake.

Yes, I keep watch for you while you stay awake elsewhere—far off from me, but all too close to others.

Note: Chief among the ambiguities of the *Sonnets* are phrases like *my love*: it can of course mean my love for you, or you who are my love, or the love you have for me. Such ambiguities force the serious reader to be interactive.

Sin of self-love possesseth all mine eye,
And all my soul and all my every part;
And for this sin there is no remedy,
It is so grounded inward in my heart.
Methinks no face so gracious is as mine,
No shape so true, no truth of such account,
And for myself mine own worth do define,
As I all other in all worths surmount.
But when my glass shows me myself indeed,
Beated and chopped with tanned antiquity,
Mine own self-love quite contrary I read;
Self so self-loving were iniquity.
'Tis thee, myself, that for myself I praise,
Painting my age with beauty of thy days.

AN EXCUSE FOR MY SELF-LOVE

THE SINFUL LOVE of self obsesses me, infects my eyes, my soul, and all the rest of me. There's no cure for it, so deeply is it embedded in my bones.

I think no face is so handsome as mine, no body so well-proportioned, no qualities of such value. I myself measure my worth, and find it excelling all others in every respect.

But when the mirror shows me my true self—worn and cracked and leathery with age—I get an opposite reading on my self-love: self-love is bad enough, but to love such a self would indeed be a crime.

But since I identify my aging self with your youthful beauty, it is you, my true self, that I am praising when I laud myself.

Note: L8: *other*: others. / This sonnet begins with one of the 8 *sins*; there are also 3 *sinfuls*. Related words abound: *shame* (14), *wrong* (9), *crime* (4), *fault* (3), *trespass* (2), *transgression* and *iniquity* (1 each); also, *evil* as a noun (4), *bad* (7), and *vice* (2). Given these frequencies, the single appearance of *guilt* is striking, though *disgrace* has 9 occurrences, *penance* and *repent*, one each. There is no "regret" or "remorse." There is a single *devil* (and a single *saint*), but no "Satan" or "demon." / See S29 for a different self-appraisal.

63

*A*gainst my love shall be, as I am now,
  With Time's injurious hand crushed and
    o'erworn;
When hours have drained his blood and filled his
  brow
With lines and wrinkles; when his youthful morn
Hath travelled on to age's steepy night,
And all those beauties whereof now he's king
Are vanishing, or vanished out of sight,
Stealing away the treasure of his spring:
For such a time do I now fortify
Against confounding age's cruel knife,
That he shall never cut from memory
My sweet love's beauty, though my lover's life.
  His beauty shall in these black lines be seen,
  And they shall live, and he in them still green.

BLACK INK WILL KEEP
MY LOVER GREEN

AGAINST THE DAY when my beloved will be
as I am now—bashed and beaten down by time's
lacerating hand; when the passing hours have
thinned his blood, and thickened his brow with
lines and wrinkles; when his morning of youth has
journeyed on to the night of sudden aging; when all
the beauties of which he is now king will be fading
or already faded from view—a loss which will steal
away the treasures of his springtime.

Foreseeing such a day I build a defense
against the cruel blade of frustrating age, so that
it will never cut from memory my sweet love's
winsomeness, even though it cuts away his life.

His beauty shall be captured in these inky lines.
These shall live on, and through them will he stay
forever green.

Note: Ls 4, 13: facial lines will be undone by written lines. / Ls 7, 9: the steel knife
of aging will steal away treasures. / The very first sonnet mentions the key word
memory, cited 7 times later, here and elsewhere. *Remember* makes 2 explicit
appearances, along with *forget* (10), *memorial*, and *oblivion* (1 each).

64

When I have seen by Time's fell hand defac'd

The rich proud cost of outworn buried age;

When sometime lofty towers I see down-raz'd

And brass eternal slave to mortal rage;

When I have seen the hungry ocean gain

Advantage on the kingdom of the shore,

And the firm soil win of the watery main,

Increasing store with loss, and loss with store;

When I have seen such interchange of state,

Or state itself confounded to decay;

Ruin hath taught me thus to ruminate

That Time will come and take my love away.

    This thought is as a death, which cannot choose

    But weep to have that which it fears to lose.

IT IS A FEARFUL THING TO LOVE/WHAT DEATH CAN TOUCH.

—Gravestone in Whitefield, N.H.

I HAVE SEEN the sinister hand of Time deface the proud, costly monuments entombing the remains of shriveled elders.

I have seen once lofty towers cut down, and so-called ever-lasting brass destroyed by human rage.

I've seen the hungry ocean eat away at the kingdom of the shore, or else land advancing at the expense of the sea—one side gaining from the other's loss, or losing by the other's gain.

I've seen these interchanges of parts, or even the whole itself collapsing away.

Such ruinations have taught me to face the fact that Time will come and take my beloved away. This thought itself is like a death, and the thinker cannot help but weep, possessing what he fears he may lose at any moment.

N ote: Time giveth and time taketh away. Is it blessed? / L1: *fell*: sinister; related to felon (whose root is "wicked"). By contrast, in Jesuit Gerard Manley Hopkins' sonnet, "I wake and feel the fell of dark not day," "fell" means an animal hide.

65

Since brass, nor stone, nor earth, nor boundless
    sea,
But sad mortality o'ersways their power,
How with this rage shall beauty hold a plea,
Whose action is no stronger than a flower?
O how shall summer's honey breath hold out
Against the wreckful siege of battering days,
When rocks impregnable are not so stout,
Nor gates of steel so strong, but Time decays?
O! fearful meditation! where, alack,
Shall Time's best jewel from Time's chest lie hid?
Or what strong hand can hold his swift foot back,
Or who his spoil of beauty can forbid?
    O! none, unless this miracle have might,
    That in black ink my love may still shine bright.

CAN DARK INK ENSURE A BRIGHT FUTURE?

THE TRAGEDY OF DEATH overwhelms the power of brass and stone and earth and infinite sea. Against such fury, then, what hope is there for beauty, whose force is no stronger than a flower?

How will summer's honeyed breath hold out against the destructive siege of battering winds, when not even impregnable rocks and gates of steel are strong enough to fight off Time's decay?

This is a terrifying thought! Where, alas, can you who are Time's best jewel be hidden from Time's casket? What strong hand can hold back Time's swift foot, or who can forbid it to seize your beauty as its spoil?

No one, unless by some mighty miracle my beloved may glow ever brightly in the black of ink.

Note: This sonnet is a twin of S64, and expands its thought into a meditation, a rumination on ruin. It makes a chilling, unexpected play on the idea of a casket.

66

*T*ired with all these, for restful death I cry
    As to behold desert a beggar born,
And needy nothing trimm'd in jollity,
And purest faith unhappily forsworn,
And gilded honour shamefully misplac'd,
And maiden virtue rudely strumpeted,
And right perfection wrongfully disgrac'd,
And strength by limping sway disabled,
And art made tongue-tied by authority,
And folly, doctor-like, controlling skill,
And simple truth miscall'd simplicity,
And captive good attending captain ill:
    Tired with all these, from these would I be gone,
    Save that to die, I leave my love alone.

A BILL OF COMPLAINTS

I BEG FOR untroubled death because I'm tired of things like these:

- deserving people born into beggary, while empty, worthless people don their gay apparel;
- the purest faith wretchedly betrayed, while golden honors are shamefully misbestowed;
- maiden chastity crudely defamed or violated;
- genuine excellence visited with wrongful shame;
- the strong disabled by disabled authority;
- art made tongue-tied by censors;
- foolish teachers in charge of the truly gifted;
- simple truth branded as simple-mindedness;
- and captive good enslaved to captain evil.

Weary of all of this, I'd gladly be gone, except that by dying I'd leave my beloved alone.

Note: S66 may be borrowing its pessimism from the biblically ominous number "666" (*Revelation* 15:18). / L3: *needy nothing*: nobodies lacking all gifts. / L8: there may be specific political events intended here: strong men cannot outwit even a weak government. / L10: *doctor*: Ph.D., not M.D.

67

Ah! wherefore with infection should he live,
And with his presence grace impiety,
That sin by him advantage should achieve,
And lace itself with his society?
Why should false painting imitate his cheek,
And steal dead seeing of his living hue?
Why should poor beauty indirectly seek
Roses of shadow, since his Rose is true?
Why should he live, now Nature bankrupt is,
Beggar'd of blood to blush through lively veins,
For she hath no exchequer now but his,
And, proud of many, lives upon his gains.
   O! him she stores, to show what wealth she had
   In days long since, before these last so bad.

WHY THE BELOVED IS ALIVE IN A DEAD WORLD

WHY SHOULD MY BELOVED continue living in a world so infected, and by his presence reflect some grace on wickedness? Corrupt people gain thereby some advantage through him, and trim themselves with the lace of his companionship.

Why should deceitful cosmetics try to imitate his face, and steal a lifeless hue from his living color? Why should ungifted faces thus deviously seek to attain a false Rosiness, when the Rose of his beauty is genuine?

Why should he live on, now that Nature is bankrupt and has no more ideal blood to send blushing through living veins? She has invested her all in him. Having once flourished in many other worthy souls, she now lives solely through his attainments.

Nature keeps him alive to show what resources she had in days long since, before these rotten times.

Note: References to *Roses, beauty,* and *dead* recall the first sentence of S1. The life-weary poet seems oddly ambivalent about the fact that his ideal lover continues living in a world so far from ideal. Indeed, the beloved seems somehow complicit in the evils of the day.

*T*hus is his cheek the map of days outworn,
    When beauty liv'd and died as flowers do
      now,
Before the bastard signs of fair were born,
Or durst inhabit on a living brow;
Before the golden tresses of the dead,
The right of sepulchres, were shorn away,
To live a second life on second head;
Ere beauty's dead fleece made another gay:
In him those holy antique hours are seen,
Without all ornament, itself and true,
Making no summer of another's green,
Robbing no old to dress his beauty new;
    And him as for a map doth Nature store,
    To show false Art what beauty was of yore.

BEAUTY OLDEN AND GOLDEN

MY BELOVED'S FACE is a map of former days, when human beauty lived and died as naturally as flowers do.

That was before wigs were born and other bastard signs of beauty dared to dwell on a living brow; before the golden locks of the dead, owed to tombs, were shaved away to live a second life on a second skull; before beauty's dead fleece made another person seem more alive.

In my beloved, those holy, antique times are revived, when beauty was itself and true, free of false ornament designed to make a summer out of another's green, and rob older beauty to make itself young.

Yes, nature preserves my beloved as a model, to show false art what beauty was in bygone days.

Note: This sonnet closely resembles S67. / L1: *Thus*: as a result of nature's decision in the previous sonnet. / The poet was wise to delay publishing this sonnet while he was a resident in the wig-making center of London, and Queen Elizabeth was the most famous wig-wearer in England. Almost all pictures of W.S. show him balding, so he might have been sensitive to the falsity of wigs.

69

*T*hose parts of thee that the world's eye doth
      view

Want nothing that the thought of hearts can mend;

All tongues, the voice of souls, give thee that due,

Uttering bare truth, even so as foes commend.

Thy outward thus with outward praise is crown'd,

But those same tongues that give thee so thine own,

In other accents do this praise confound

By seeing farther than the eye hath shown.

They look into the beauty of thy mind,

And that in guess they measure by thy deeds;

Then, churls, their thoughts, although their eyes were
      kind,

To thy fair flower add the rank smell of weeds:

    But why thy odour matcheth not thy show,

    The soil is this, that thou dost common grow.

IS VULGAR COMPANY CORRUPTING YOU?

THOSE ASPECTS OF YOU which the world's eye can see lack nothing that imagination could improve upon. Voicing what the soul sees, every tongue grants you this flawlessness, and utters this plain truth as even your enemies would. Your outward charm is thus crowned with outward praise.

But those same tongues, while thus granting you your due, negate this praise with other comments when their minds look deeper than their eyes can probe.

They wonder about the beauty of your soul, and make guesses based on your deeds. Though their eyes were kind, their churlish thoughts are now ungenerous, and attribute to your flowering beauty the stench of rotten weeds.

Why does your fragrance not match your appearance? The ground for complaint is that you are becoming vulgar like your hangers-on.

Note: This sonnet recalls the prayer of Socrates, "that the outward and inner man should be at one." (Plato's *Phaedrus*.) / A key idea in the *Sonnets* is the deceptiveness of appearances. That deceit is also operative when beauty which seems so pure holds within itself the very seeds of ugliness.

70

That thou art blam'd shall not be thy defect,
For slander's mark was ever yet the fair;
The ornament of beauty is suspect,
A crow that flies in heaven's sweetest air.
So thou be good, slander doth but approve
Thy worth the greater, being woo'd of time;
For canker vice the sweetest buds doth love,
And thou present'st a pure unstained prime.
Thou hast passed by the ambush of young days,
Either not assailed, or victor being charged;
Yet this thy praise cannot be so thy praise,
To tie up envy, evermore enlarged:

    If some suspect of ill masked not thy show,
    Then thou alone kingdoms of hearts shouldst owe.

QUALITY BEGETS ENVY AND SLANDER

IT ISN'T YOUR FAULT that you are blamed. Beautiful people have always been the target of slander; indeed, like an ugly crow flying in heaven's sweetest air, suspicion is a very ornament of beauty.

As long as you are truly good, slander merely proves the exceptional worth which people are currently courting in you. A vicious canker loves the sweetest buds, but you in your prime shine pure and unstained.

Either unattacked or victorious when attacked, you have passed beyond the ambushes of your younger days. Yet this achievement of yours is not so successful that it can confine the envy which is always expanding. If some suspicion of evil did not cloud what you seem to be, you by yourself would possess whole kingdoms of hearts.

Note: L4: *crow*: in 1592 the dying playwright Robert Greene wrote a first and rare attack on W.S., then in his late 20s. Dubbing him "Shake-scene," Greene mocked his plays and branded him an "upstart crow" who beautifies himself with others' feathers. Greene's publisher, Henry Chettle, soon printed a revealing apology. He himself found W.S. "civil and excellent"; moreover, "divers of worship" (a variety of worthy folk) commended his uprightness, honesty, and literary grace.

71

No longer mourn for me when I am dead
  Then you shall hear the surly sullen bell
Give warning to the world that I am fled
From this vile world, with vilest worms to dwell;
Nay, if you read this line, remember not
The hand that writ it, for I love you so
That I in your sweet thoughts would be forgot,
If thinking on me then should make you woe.
O! if, I say, you look upon this verse
When I perhaps compounded am with clay,
Do not so much as my poor name rehearse,
But let your love even with my life decay;
  Lest the wise world should look into your moan,
  And mock you with me after I am gone.

WHEN I AM DEAD, MY DEAREST, SING NO SAD SONGS FOR ME

—*Christina Rossetti*

WHEN I DIE, beloved, don't mourn for me any longer than it takes the tolling bell, sour and gloomy, to warn the world that I have fled its vileness to dwell with vilest worms.

Indeed, if you ever read this sonnet, forget the hand that wrote it. For I love you so much that I would rather be absent from your sweet thoughts if remembering me would make you sad.

As I said, if you gaze on these lines when I am mixed with clay, don't so much as repeat my name. Let your love for me decay as my body does, lest the worldly-wise pry into your sadness and tease you about my unworthiness.

Note: Psalm 90 speaks of 70 years as the typical life span. Now past 70 in number, this sonnet and the 3 that follow take a post-mortem view. / L2: 2 years before *Shakespeare's Sonnets* was published, the poet paid for the tolling of the bells at the London funeral of his actor brother, Edmund. / L3's *warning* is possibly facetious: "Dead, I can now haunt." / Ls 6–8: Christina Rossetti (1830–94), who wrote the epigram above, added in another poem: "Better by far you should forget and smile,/Than that you should remember and be sad." / The *world*, which occurs thrice here, has 29 other appearances in the *Sonnets*. Most often it just means people in general. Though the *public* occurs thrice and *society* once, there is no "people" or "folk."

O! *lest the world should task you to recite*
　　What merit lived in me, that you should
　　love,
After my death, dear love, forget me quite,
For you in me can nothing worthy prove;
Unless you would devise some virtuous lie
To do more for me than mine own desert,
And hang more praise upon deceased I
Than niggard truth would willingly impart:
O! lest your true love may seem false in this,
That you for love speak well of me untrue,
My name be buried where my body is,
And live no more to shame nor me nor you.
　　For I am shamed by that which I bring forth,
　　And so should you, to love things nothing worth.

NO LOVING LIES,
WHEN DEAD I LIE

AFTER MY DEATH, dearly beloved, forget me completely. Otherwise people will challenge you to spell out why I merit your posthumous love.

You won't be able to give a worthy reason—unless you invent some virtuous lie to ennoble me more than I deserve, to adorn me with more praise than strict honesty would willingly confer.

Rather than have your true love seem false by lovingly speaking well of me (but untruly), let my name be buried where my body lies. Let it live no longer to shame either me or you.

For I am embarrassed by what I produce, as you should be to love what is worthless.

Note: Can this be the same poet who vaunted his own skill, and promised to immortalize the Fair Youth through poetry? / Ls 9–14: with 4 exceptions, the last 6 lines of this sonnet (60 syllables) contain nothing but monosyllables—words which are usually ancient, Anglo-Saxon words close to the senses, daily life, and rich earthiness. (Note how many words for body parts are only a single syllable.) About 80 percent of *Shakespeare's Sonnets* consists of monosyllables, especially the final couplets.

*T*hat time of year thou mayst in me behold
　　When yellow leaves, or none, or few, do hang
Upon those boughs which shake against the cold,
Bare ruined choirs, where late the sweet birds sang.
In me thou seest the twilight of such day
As after sunset fadeth in the west,
Which by and by black night doth take away,
Death's second self, that seals up all in rest.
In me thou seest the glowing of such fire
That on the ashes of his youth doth lie,
As the death-bed whereon it must expire,
Consumed with that which it was nourished by.

　　This thou perceiv'st, which makes thy love more strong,

　　　To love that well which thou must leave ere long.

THE REASON WHY
I CLASP THEM IS,
THEY DIE

—WILLIAM CORY

IN ME YOU CAN SEE an image of that time of year when a few yellow leaves, or none at all, hang on branches shivering from the cold. The limbs seem like bare, ruined choir stalls where recently sweet birds sang like monks.

Again, I'm like the twilight of the day, after the sunlight fades in the west. Gradually the black of night takes over, a twin of the death that seals up everything in repose.

I'm like the glow of a fire that rests on the ashes of its former self. These are the deathbed of the expiring flame: the wood that fed that flame will now swallow it up.

You understand all of this, and it strengthens your love. You want to love well what you will soon lose.

Note: Ls 13–14: unless these lines refer to the Youth's inevitable loss of youth and sexual potency (and if they do, they are the only *carpe diem* hint in *SS*), it seems odd that in this glorious sonnet W.S. tells his friend what the friend is feeling about him, and why, and speaks of the friend as the one who is leaving. / Titchfield House, the chief country home of the Catholic Southamptons, was built from the ruins of a monastery. W.S. was a frequent guest. H.W.'s mother, Dowager Countess Mary, boldly hid fugitive priests in her London home.

But be contented when that fell arrest
  Without all bail shall carry me away,
My life hath in this line some interest,
Which for memorial still with thee shall stay.
When thou reviewest this, thou dost review
The very part was consecrate to thee:
The earth can have but earth, which is his due;
My spirit is thine, the better part of me.
So then thou hast but lost the dregs of life,
The prey of worms, my body being dead,
The coward conquest of a wretch's knife,
Too base of thee to be remembered:
    The worth of that is that which it contains,
    And that is this, and this with thee remains.

THE BEST OF ME, THE REST OF ME

DON'T BE TROUBLED! When death's dire arrest-warrant carts me off with no hope of bail, my life will still earn interest through these lines, a memorial which will stay behind with you.

Moreover, when you visit these lines, you will be revisiting that part of me which was consecrated to you. As is its due, earth will claim my earthiness. But my spirit is yours, and that's the better part of me.

When my body is dead, you will have lost something too base for you to remember—the mere dregs of my existence, the victim feast of worms, the trophy of Death the Wretch and his cowardly stiletto.

The value of that body lay in the creativity it housed. These resultant sonnets are the true remains which will remain with you.

Note: L1: the opening *But* implies a link with the previous sonnet. Two sonnets ago, the poet said,"Forget me and my embarrassing poems." Preparing for death, people sometimes change their wills. / L11: readers have variously seen in this "cowardly knife" the murder of Kit Marlowe, a would-be assassin, or W.S. contemplating suicide.

*S*o are you to my thoughts as food to life,
  Or as sweet-seasoned showers are to the
    ground;
And for the peace of you I hold such strife
As 'twixt a miser and his wealth is found:
Now proud as an enjoyer and anon
Doubting the filching age will steal his treasure;
Now counting best to be with you alone,
Then bettered that the world may see my pleasure;
Sometime all full with feasting on your sight,
And by and by clean starved for a look;
Possessing or pursuing no delight
Save what is had or must from you be took.
    Thus do I pine and surfeit day by day,
    Or gluttoning on all, or all away.

YOU ARE EITHER A FEAST OR A FAST

YOU ARE TO MY THOUGHTS what food is to life, or sweet seasonal showers to parched soil. But when it comes to the peace your presence brings me, I am in the kind of conflict a miser feels toward his wealth: proud to enjoy it but worried that, if he proudly exhibits his treasures, the thieving times will steal them.

At one moment, my being alone with you seems the better arrangement. In the next, it seems preferable that the outside world should behold what delights me. At times I am bloated from feasting on the sight of you. Later I am quite ravenous for a look.

Enjoying your presence or needing what only you can provide, I have no pleasure except to possess you or pursue you. Thus day by day I fast or feast. Either I gluttonize on your abundance or face a total famine.

Note: H.W.'s patronage of W.S. was literally food for his life at a time when plague shut down London theaters. Dedicating *Venus and Adonis* to him, the poet left us the first of his few surviving personal remarks. The 135 words begin: "I know not how I shall offend in dedicating my unpolished lines to your lordship, nor how the world will censure me for choosing so strong a prop to support so weak a burden." One rumor said that H.W. replied with an unlikely thousand pounds.

76

Why is my verse so barren of new pride,
        So far from variation or quick change?
Why with the time do I not glance aside
To new-found methods and to compounds strange?
Why write I still all one, ever the same,
And keep invention in a noted weed,
That every word doth almost tell my name,
Showing their birth and where they did proceed?
O! know, sweet love, I always write of you,
And you and love are still my argument;
So all my best is dressing old words new,
Spending again what is already spent:
        For as the sun is daily new and old,
        So is my love still telling what is told.

WHY I AM A WILLIE-ONE-NOTE

WHY, BELOVED, ARE these sonnets so empty of clever novelties, so lacking in variety and sudden shifts? Why don't I follow fashion and imitate the latest methods, or coin strange combinations of words?

Why is my writing all of a piece, ever the same? Its creativity is dressed in a recognizable style—so that almost every line bears my signature, revealing who inspired it and who received it.

Realize this, sweet love: I'm always writing about you. You and love are my constant themes. The best I can do is to robe old words in new garments, and spend coins of invention that I have already spent.

Just as the sun is new and old every day, so is my love always proclaiming what it has already proclaimed.

Note: L6: *noted weed*: recognizable clothing. / L10: *still*: always. The poet here seems to be patiently chiding the shallow objections of the Youth and his taste for novelty. The poet was as inventive as they come, and his interest in opulence of style was extraordinary. But, deep writers require deep readers.

*T*hy glass will show thee how thy beauties
    wear,
Thy dial how thy precious minutes waste,
The vacant leaves thy mind's imprint will bear,
And of this book, this learning mayst thou taste.
The wrinkles which thy glass will truly show
Of mouthed graves will give thee memory;
Thou by thy dial's shady stealth mayst know
Time's thievish progress to eternity.
Look! what thy memory cannot contain
Commit to these waste blanks, and thou shalt find
Those children nursed, delivered from thy brain,
To take a new acquaintance of thy mind.
    These offices, so oft as thou wilt look,
    Shall profit thee, and much enrich thy book.

VACANT SPACES CAN FURNISH YOUR MIND

YOUR MIRROR WILL show you how much your charms are wilting. The moving hands of your clock will remind you how your precious minutes are ticking away. The blank pages of this gift journal will now reveal your own thoughts about mortality. From this book of sonnets too you may get a taste of the mortal truth.

The wrinkles candidly revealed by your mirror will remind you of opened graves. The shady stealth of clock hands will proclaim Time's thieving passage from here to eternity.

As for this new journal, here's my advice: Commit to its blank pages whatever you are in danger of forgetting. You will learn that if you feed these brain-children by pondering on them, they in turn will increase your self-knowledge.

Every time you practice these exercises, you will stand to gain personally, and your journal will become that much more valuable.

Note: Four reminders of death: the mirror, the clock, your journal, my sonnets. Experts disagree as to whether the Youth is being urged to write his own thoughts in a new journal, or to add commentary in the vacant spaces surrounding the sonnets—or both. In any case, it would be the Youth's own thoughts, not W.S.'s, which would now benefit him.

So oft have I invoked thee for my Muse,
    And found such fair assistance in my verse,
As every Alien *pen hath got my use,*
And under thee their poesy disperse.
Thine eyes, that taught the dumb on high to sing,
And heavy ignorance aloft to fly,
Have added feathers to the learned's wing
And given grace a double majesty.
Yet be most proud of that which I compile,
Whose influence is thine, and born of thee:
In others' works thou dost but mend the style,
And arts with thy sweet graces graced be;
    But thou art all my art and dost advance
    As high as learning my rude ignorance.

MY VERSES VERSUS THEIRS

I HAVE, BELOVED, so often invoked you as my Muse, and found in you such inspiration for my poetry, that every strange pen has adopted my practice and circulated its poems under your patronage.

In my case, your eyes have taught the mute to sing on high, and given flight to weighty ignorance. Now those eyes have added feathers to the wings of the learned, and made gracefulness doubly graceful.

But, please, be proudest of what I have composed. For your influence brought about the very birth of my efforts. In the writings of others you have merely improved the style, or by your sweet graces added grace to art.

My art, by contrast, owes everything to you. You have elevated my rough knowledge to the highest level of learning.

Note: L3: *Alien*: a key candidate for being "W.H.," H.W. had a resident tutor who was a fertile writer—the Italian John Florio. He was also an informer for the Earl's guardian, Lord Burghley. (See S125's *suborned informer.*) Florio's wife is sometimes proposed as the Dark Lady of the final 28 sonnets. See S138 for other nominees. / L14: here W.S. seems to admit that he lacked the learning of the so-called "university wits," such as Kit Marlowe.

79

*W*hilst I alone did call upon thy aid,
  My verse alone had all thy gentle grace,
But now my gracious numbers are decayed
And my sick Muse doth give another place.
I grant, sweet love, thy lovely argument
Deserves the travail of a worthier pen,
Yet what of thee thy poet doth invent
He robs thee of and pays it thee again:
He lends thee virtue, and he stole that word
From thy behaviour; beauty doth he give,
And found it in thy cheek; he can afford
No praise to thee but what in thee doth live.
  Then thank him not for that which he doth say,
  Since what he owes thee, thou thyself dost pay.

MY SUPERIOR RIVAL
MERITS NO THANKS

WHEN I WAS THE ONLY poet invoking your patronage, my poems alone reflected all your gentle grace. But now my graceful verses are failing, and my ailing Muse yields place to another poet's Muse.

I agree, sweet love, that the theme of your loveliness deserves the labor of a worthier pen. But whatever this new poet creates, he robs from you and then pays you back with it.

He attributes "virtue" to you, but he stole the very word from your behavior. He confers on you the beauty he already found in your face. There is no praise he can apply to you that he didn't see exemplified in you.

Do not thank him, then, for what he says. You yourself pay the price of anything with which he claims to embellish you.

Note: Here first appears the theme of a specific rival poet. Guesses as to his identity include Kit Marlowe (1564–93), Ben Jonson (1572–1637), and George Chapman (c.1559–1634). Chapman's translation of Homer inspired John Keats (1795–1821) to write his famous sonnet, *On First Looking into Chapman's Homer*: "Much have I travell'd in the realms of gold..."

80

O! how I faint when I of you do write,
   Knowing a better spirit doth use your
   name,
And in the praise thereof spends all his might,
To make me tongue-tied, speaking of your fame!
But since your worth, wide as the ocean is,
The humble as the proudest sail doth bear,
My saucy bark, inferior far to his,
On your broad main doth wilfully appear.
Your shallowest help will hold me up afloat,
Whilst he upon your soundless deep doth ride,
Or, being wracked, I am a worthless boat,
He of tall building and of goodly pride.
   Then if he thrive and I be cast away,
   The worst was this: my love was my decay.

MY MAN-OF-WAR
VERSUS HIS GALLEON

I GET WEAK in the knees now when I write about you! I know that a better poet is invoking your name and going full blast at praising you. That development makes me tongue-tied when I would talk of your glory.

But your excellence is as wide as the ocean, with room enough for both the humblest and the proudest vessel. So, though my saucy skiff is far inferior to his, it takes its wilful place on your broad expanse.

Your shallowest parts are all the depth I need to stay afloat, while he rides upon your unsounded deep. If I crack up, I'm just a trifling boat, while he has loftiness and noble self-assurance.

Still, if he thrives in your affection and I am thrown aside, this will be the worst of it: it was my very love that was my undoing.

Note: Small English ships famously defeated the Spanish galleons of the 1588 Armada—a recent memory when W.S. was writing his sonnets. A later comparison likened Ben Jonson to "a Spanish great galleon built far higher in learning; solid, but slow...Shake-spear, like the English man-of-war, lesser in bulk, but lighter in sailing, could turn with all tides, tack about, and take advantage of all winds, by the quickness of his wit and invention." (Thomas Fuller, 1662)

81

Or I shall live your epitaph to make,
 Or you survive when I in earth am rotten,
From hence your memory death cannot take,
Although in me each part will be forgotten.
Your name from hence immortal life shall have,
Though I, once gone, to all the world must die;
The earth can yield me but a common grave,
When you entombed in men's eyes shall lie.
Your monument shall be my gentle verse,
Which eyes not yet created shall o'er-read,
And tongues to be your being shall rehearse,
When all the breathers of this world are dead;
  You still shall live, such virtue hath my pen,
  Where breath most breathes, even in the mouths
of men.

POSTHUMOUS VARIABLES

EITHER I WILL SURVIVE to write your epitaph, or you will be living when I am rotting in the ground. In either case, death cannot take away your memory from my book of poems, though everything about me will be forgotten. From its pages your name shall win life eternal, though once I am gone I will be dead to all the world.

The earth can grant me only a common grave, but you will lie entombed in readers' eyes. Your monument will be my tender verses: eyes not yet created will read them; tongues not yet existing will talk about your life when all who are now breathing on this planet have vanished.

Such is the power of my pen that you will always be living where breath is most alive—on the tongues of human beings.

Note: Though S81 shows W.S. both humble and pen-proud, he got things exactly backwards. Almost 5 centuries after his death, his grave draws 3 million visitors a year; his name and works are revered by hundreds of millions. But who has ever much admired the Youth, or even known who he was or where he is buried? / The first of 4 *graves* appeared in S1, the first of 6 *tombs* in S3; here we have both. Also starting in S1, *burial* occurs 5 times, with an implied one here.

I grant thou wert not married to my Muse,
And therefore mayst without attaint o'erlook
The dedicated words which writers use
Of their fair subject, blessing every book.
Thou art as fair in knowledge as in hue,
Finding thy worth a limit past my praise,
And therefore art enforced to seek anew
Some fresher stamp of the time-bettering days.
And do so, love; yet when they have devised
What strained touches rhetoric can lend,
Thou, truly fair, wert truly sympathized
In true plain words by thy true-telling friend;
   And their gross painting might be better used
   Where cheeks need blood; in thee it is abused.

BETTER POETS: NEEDED BUT NOT NOTED

I ADMIT THAT you did not exchange vows with my Muse. Therefore, without taint of adultery, you can peruse the words which other writers dedicate to your handsomeness, and endorse every book written about you.

Since your intelligence matches your beauty, you realize that your gifts excel my capacity to celebrate them. Consequently you are forced to seek some fresher voices distinguished with the latest improvements in style. Please do so, beloved.

But when they have figured out which forced phrases to add to your portrait, remember that your true beauty was truly captured in true, plain words by your truth-telling friend.

These other poets would be better employed to devote their excesses to bloodless cheeks. In your case, such touching up is an abuse.

Note: Ls 11–12: W.S. loved to play with words, whence the quartet of *trues* in two lines. Such play was common in sonnets.

83

I never saw that you did painting need,
And therefore to your fair no painting set;
I found (or thought I found) you did exceed
The barren tender of a poet's debt:
And therefore have I slept in your report,
That you yourself, being extant, well might show
How far a modern quill doth come too short,
Speaking of worth, what worth in you doth grow.
This silence for my sin you did impute,
Which shall be most my glory, being dumb,
For I impair not beauty, being mute,
When others would give life, and bring a tomb.
 There lives more life in one of your fair eyes
 Than both your poets can in praise devise.

MUST MY SILENT PEN DO PENANCE?

IT NEVER OCCURRED to me that you needed any cosmetics; that's why I applied none to your beauty. I found (or thought I did) that your excellence surpassed the sterile duties of a poet.

Therefore I have been sleeping on the job of describing you. But this was how I figured: since you are still alive, you could embarrassingly reveal how far short a modern quill comes if it tries to describe the kind of qualities blossoming in you.

You, however, consider my reticence a sin. But it will be to my supreme glory that I refused to use a modern style. My muteness brings no harm to your loveliness, whereas other poets kill by trying to enliven.

There is more life in one of your sparkling eyes than both your poets could suggest with all their praising.

Note: L3: *or thought I found*: a putdown? / L14: *both your poets*: W.S. and his chief poetic rival?

84

ho is it that says most, which can say
    more

Than this rich praise—that you alone are you,

In whose confine immured is the store

Which should example where your equal grew?

Lean penury within that pen doth dwell

That to his subject lends not some small glory,

But he that writes of you, if he can tell

That you are you, so dignifies his story.

Let him but copy what in you is writ,

Not making worse what nature made so clear,

And such a counterpart shall fame his wit,

Making his style admired every where.

    You to your beauteous blessings add a curse,

    Being fond on praise, which makes your praises

worse.

THE PLAIN TRUTH
IS ENOUGH

WHICH POET SAYS the most about you? Which can speak richer praise than this: you are unique. Within the abundance of your self is the full store of whatever comparisons would be worthy of you.

That pen is surely weak which cannot add some small glory to its subject. But he who writes about you will glorify his subject if he can merely reveal that you are you.

Let him but copy what is already inscribed in you, and not obscure what nature made so clear. Such a reproduction will bring fame to his genius and make his style universally admired.

You, however, put a hex on your lovely blessings by craving for praise. Those who would feed that hunger only make their would-be praises more artificial.

Note: After repeatedly rhapsodizing about the Fair Youth's qualities, the poet suddenly becomes a Dutch uncle and chastises him for his love of the very kind of praise this sonnet is now according him. / *Praise* is a busy word in the *Sonnets*, where it makes 28 appearances—averaging one occurrence in every five sonnets.

85

*M*y tongue-tied Muse in manners holds her
    still,

While comments of your praise, richly compiled,

Reserve their character with golden quill

And precious phrase by all the Muses filed.

I think good thoughts, whilst other write good words,

And, like unlettered clerk, still cry "Amen"

To every hymn that able spirit affords

In polished form of well-refined pen.

Hearing you praised, I say "'Tis so," "'tis true,"

And to the most of praise add something more;

But that is in my thought, whose love to you,

Though words come hindmost, holds his rank before.

Then others for the breath of words respect,

Me for my dumb thoughts, speaking in effect.

MY SILENCE SPEAKS LOUDER THAN WORDS

MY DUMBFOUNDED MUSE modestly maintains her silence while others pile on statements of praise to immortalize your character with golden pen and polished phrases inspired by all the Muses.

I think good thoughts while others write good words. Like an illiterate clergyman, I keep crying "Amen!" to every hymn which any gifted poet composes in the polished style of a well-trained quill. Hearing you praised, I answer, "It's right! It's true!" and thereby add something more to the utmost praise.

But that response occurs in my thoughts, the thoughts of one whose love for you is foremost, though his words come hindmost.

Esteem others, then, for the words they utter. Respect me for my mute thoughts, which find their voice in actions.

Note: The picture of a verbally-deprived cleric shouting "Amen!" to every hymn provides the *Sonnets* with a rare comic note. Its few competitors are the instant limping in S89, and the housewife chasing a chicken in S143. / Ls 6–7: this is the only *clerk* and *hymn* in the *Sonnets*, though a lark and a nightingale get to sing *hymns*.

86

Was it the proud full sail of his great verse,
  Bound for the prize of all too precious
    you,
That did my ripe thoughts in my brain inhearse,
Making their tomb the womb wherein they grew?
Was it his spirit, by spirits taught to write
Above a mortal pitch, that struck me dead?
No, neither he, nor his compeers by night
Giving him aid, my verse astonished.
He, nor that affable familiar ghost
Which nightly gulls him with intelligence
As victors of my silence cannot boast;
I was not sick of any fear from thence:
  But when your countenance filled up his line,
  Then lacked I matter; that enfeebled mine.

MY RIVAL STOLE ALL MY MATERIAL

WHAT WAS IT that buried my ripe thoughts in my brain, and made thereby a tomb of the womb where they grew?

Was it the proud full sail of my rival's lofty verse, bounty hunting for the booty of your most priceless self? Was I struck dumb by his genius, taught as it is by ghostly spirits how to write better than any mortal?

No, my verse was stunned into silence neither by him nor by the nocturnal spirits that lend him aid. No, neither he nor that friendly familiar ghost that nightly tricks him with false information can boast that they silenced me. I was not weakened by any such sources.

But when I beheld your approving face appropriated in his every line, I had no subject left to revive my exhausted verses.

Note: As mentioned concerning S79, there are various guesses as to who this other poet was. What of these night visitors? Another puzzle. Chapman claimed to converse with Homer. In his *Tragical History of Dr. Faustus*, Kit Marlowe dramatized the story of a man who sells his soul for help from hell in the person of Mephistopheles. Presumably the latter made night calls.

87

Farewell! thou art too dear for my possessing,
And like enough thou know'st thy estimate:
The charter of thy worth gives thee releasing;
My bonds in thee are all determinate.
For how do I hold thee but by thy granting?
And for that riches where is my deserving?
The cause of this fair gift in me is wanting,
And so my patent back again is swerving.
Thy self thou gav'st, thy own worth then not knowing,
Or me, to whom thou gav'st it, else mistaking;
So thy great gift, upon misprision growing,
Comes home again, on better judgement making.
   Thus have I had thee as a dream doth flatter,
   In sleep a king, but waking no such matter.

WHY SHOULDN'T YOU WITHDRAW YOUR PATRONAGE?

GOODBYE, MY PATRON that was! You are too precious for me to monopolize. Chances are that by now you too know your true value. The privilege of your excellence permits you to dismiss me; all my claims on you have lapsed.

For how did I possess you except as a grant on your part? How could I ever earn such wealth? On my part there can be no deserving of a gift so gracious.

And so the license of your patronage reverts to you. You conferred it on me when you did not yet realize your own merit, or when you overestimated the one to whom you gave it.

So it is that your magnanimous favor goes home to you. It sprung from a misconception, and reverts as a result of wiser judgment on your part.

I possessed you as in a flattering dream. Asleep, I was a king; awake, I am no such thing.

Note: Explaining the femininity of the Youth, S20 employed all feminine rhymes. (For such rhymes, see S20.) Ten of the rhymes in this sonnet are feminine, all ending in *ing*, as does the *king* about to be deposed in L14. L10 ends with mista/*king*, L12 with ma/*king*. The poet was a master organist of the sound of words.

88

When thou shalt be disposed to set me light,
    And place my merit in the eye of scorn,
Upon thy side against myself I'll fight,
And prove thee virtuous, though thou art forsworn:
With mine own weakness being best acquainted,
Upon thy part I can set down a story
Of faults concealed wherein I am attainted,
That thou in losing me shalt win much glory;
And I by this will be a gainer too,
For, bending all my loving thoughts on thee,
The injuries that to myself I do,
Doing thee vantage, double vantage me.
    Such is my love, to thee I so belong,
    That for thy right myself will bear all wrong.

I'LL HELP YOU PIN THE BLAME ON ME

WHEN YOU ARE READY to make light of me, and gaze on my merits with a scornful eye, I'll take your side against my own, and prove you virtuous even when you perjure yourself.

Since I am better acquainted with my flaws than anyone, I can on your behalf compose a list of concealed faults that defile me. That way you will reap much credit by getting rid of me.

I myself will stand to gain thereby. Since I focus all my loving thoughts on you, the injuries I do to myself will double my advantage if they work to your advantage.

Such is my love for you, so totally am I yours, that if it makes you blameless, I'll take all the blame.

Note: Though the devotion of the poet to his friend may seem heroic, its masochistic flavor suggests the neurotic, even the pathological. But it was W.S. himself who lumped together "the lunatic, the lover, and the poet" in *A Midsummer Night's Dream* (5.1.6–8).

89

Say that thou didst forsake me for some fault,
    And I will comment upon that offence;
Speak of my lameness, and I straight will halt,
Against thy reasons making no defence.
Thou canst not, love, disgrace me half so ill,
To set a form upon desired change,
As I'll myself disgrace, knowing thy will:
I will acquaintance strangle and look strange;
Be absent from thy walks; and in my tongue
Thy sweet beloved name no more shall dwell,
Lest I, too much profane, should do it wrong,
And haply of our old acquaintance tell.
    For thee, against myself I'll vow debate,
    For I must ne'er love him whom thou dost hate.

SHOULD AULD ACQUAINTANCE BE FORGOT?

—*John Ramsay/Robert Burns*

IF YOU REJECT ME because of some offense, I will add details to the charge. If you cite my lameness, I will start limping at once, making no defense against your arguments.

As you build a case for the change you desire in our relationship, beloved, you cannot disgrace me half so much as I'll disgrace myself.

Once I know it's what you want, I will end our acquaintance and appear distant, avoiding your whereabouts. Your sweet beloved name will no longer dwell on my lips, lest I should profane and wrong it, nor will I by chance mention our former intimacy.

For your sake I swear I'll argue against myself. Never could I love the man whom you find hateful.

Note: The original title page of the *Sonnets* mentions only sonnets (though the word itself never appears in them). But the final eleven pages of the 1609 edition contain an unannounced 329-line poem entitled *A Lover's Complaint.* That section contains no sonnets, but it does speak of "deep-brained sonnets" (L209). In the poem, a young damsel laments that she has been abandoned by a dashing Don Juan. But if she got the chance, she would fall for him all over again! This present sonnet is a "complaint" or lamentation by a lover named Shakespeare.

90

*T*hen hate me when thou wilt; if ever, now,

    Now while the world is bent my deeds to cross,

Join with the spite of Fortune, make me bow,

And do not drop in for an after-loss:

Ah! do not, when my heart hath 'scaped this sorrow,

Come in the rearward of a conquered woe;

Give not a windy night a rainy morrow,

To linger out a purposed overthrow.

If thou wilt leave me, do not leave me last,

When other petty griefs have done their spite,

But in the onset come; so shall I taste

At first the very worst of Fortune's might;

    And other strains of woe, which now seem woe,

    Compared with loss of thee, will not seem so.

HATE ME NOW; DON'T BE THE LAST

HATE ME WHEN you want to, but I would prefer that you choose the present moment if any. Now, while the whole world is set on frustrating me, add to my spiteful misfortunes, bend me low. But don't let your hate arrive as an aftershock.

Since my heart has as yet escaped the pain of an explicit rejection, oh, let it not come in the wake of woes that are already overwhelming me. Do not give a windy night a rainy dawn. Do not delay any repudiation that you may be planning.

If you leave me, don't be the last to do so—after other, petty griefs have done their worst. Come in the vanguard. That way I'll feel first the worst blow of misfortune.

Then, other shocks of loss, which would now seem heavy, won't feel that way compared to my loss of you.

Note: W.S. went through strangely similar stages in his relationship with both "the man right fair" and "the woman coloured ill" (see the final 28 Ss, especially S144): formal flattery, idealization, fierce infatuation, sour disillusionment, and a sense of betrayal. Indeed, critic R. P. Blackmur finds in the *Sonnets* a "poetics of infatuation." If based on fact, the *Sonnets* were not composed by a romantic winner, but by a loser who perhaps "loved not wisely, but too well." (*Othello* 5.2.343)

91

Some glory in their birth, some in their skill,
Some in their wealth, some in their body's
force,
Some in their garments, though new-fangled ill,
Some in their hawks and hounds, some in their horse;
And every humour hath his adjunct pleasure,
Wherein it finds a joy above the rest;
But these particulars are not my measure;
All these I better in one general best.
Thy love is better than high birth to me,
Richer than wealth, prouder than garments' cost,
Of more delight than hawks or horses be;
And having thee, of all men's pride I boast:
Wretched in this alone, that thou mayst take
All this away and me most wretched make.

I HAVE EVERYTHING BUT...

SOME PEOPLE TAKE PRIDE in their ancestry, others in their skills, some in their riches, others in their physical strength, some in their wardrobe (fashionable but ugly), others in their hawks or hounds or horses. Every mood has its proper pleasure, one which brings the most delight.

But these enjoyments are not to my taste. I better all of them in one encompassing best: to me your love is higher than noble birth, richer than wealth, prouder than costly garments, more enjoyable than hawks or horses. Having you, I have everything of which other men boast.

Only one thing makes me miserable: the chance that you might take all my everything away, and make me the most bereft of all.

Note: L3: *new-fangled ill*: fashionably ugly. / A dog-loving friend noticed that the poet does not say that thy love is better even than the aforementioned hounds. / The poet from rustic Stratford is here clearly indicating that his pleasures are not those of a wealthy aristocrat.

92

But do thy worst to steal thyself away,
For term of life thou art assured mine;
And life no longer than thy love will stay,
For it depends upon that love of thine.
Then need I not to fear the worst of wrongs,
When in the least of them my life hath end;
I see a better state to me belongs
Than that which on thy humour doth depend.
Thou canst not vex me with inconstant mind,
Since that my life on thy revolt doth lie.
O! what a happy title do I find,
Happy to have thy love, happy to die!
    But what's so blessed-fair that fears no blot?
    Thou mayst be false, and yet I know it not.

YOUR LOVE'S END WILL BE MINE AS WELL

DO YOUR WORST in distancing yourself from me. You are securely mine for the rest of my life. For my life will last no longer than your love, since that life depends on your loving me. I need fear nothing that you can do, since the first hint of repudiation will put an end to my days.

I see that in death a better heritage will be mine, one which will not depend on your humors. You won't be able to torture me any longer with your changing moods, since my future will vanish if you turn against me.

What a blessed entitlement is mine, since I am happy if I have your love, and happily dead if I don't.

But what state is so beautifully blessed that it is perfectly assured? Indeed, you may have betrayed me already, without my even knowing it.

Note: Some see here the threat of suicide, and/or W.S.'s belief in an afterlife. But his imagined death could have come from shock, and he may simply be referring to a state of painless oblivion. It can't be assumed that W.S. was an orthodox Christian believer, though his father was almost surely a papist. W.S. lived in religiously dangerous times. It wasn't wise to profess one's beliefs or doubts too loudly.

93

So shall I live, supposing thou art true,
    Like a deceived husband; so love's face
May still seem love to me, though altered new;
Thy looks with me, thy heart in other place:
For there can live no hatred in thine eye,
Therefore in that I cannot know thy change.
In many's looks the false heart's history
Is writ in moods and frowns and wrinkles strange,
But heaven in thy creation did decree
That in thy face sweet love should ever dwell;
Whate'er thy thoughts or thy heart's workings be,
Thy looks should nothing thence but sweetness tell.
    How like Eve's apple doth thy beauty grow,
    If thy sweet virtue answer not thy show!

YOUR FACE IS NO CLUE

LIKE A DECEIVED HUSBAND, I'll go on living in the supposition that you are faithful. To my eyes, your face of love will keep its loving look, even if things have changed and love has departed—leaving its appearance with me, while your heart is elsewhere. For nothing hateful can dwell in your eyes. Therefore, they cannot tell me if you have changed.

In the facial expressions of many people, the story of a false heart is betrayed by moodiness and frowns and curious wrinkles. But in creating you, heaven decreed that sweet love should always dwell in your countenance.

No matter what your thoughts are, or what's going on in your heart, your looks can reveal nothing but sweetness. So, your beauty will become like Eve's deceptive apple if gracious virtue within does not match your outward appearance.

Note: L13: *Eve's* is an explicit biblical reference, as rare in the *Sonnets* as mythic ones. Whatever his personal beliefs, W.S. knew his Bible well—not the *King James Bible* (published two years after *Shakespeare's Sonnets*), but the popular yet unofficial 1560 *Geneva Bible*, issued with anti-Catholic and anti-monarchal notes by a group of English Protestant scholars. They were in exile from the England of the Catholic Queen Mary (1553–58). Even the Preface of the *KJB* quotes from it!

They that have power to hurt and will do
none,

That do not do the thing they most do show,

Who, moving others, are themselves as stone,

Unmoved, cold, and to temptation slow;

They rightly do inherit heaven's graces,

And husband nature's riches from expense;

They are the lords and owners of their faces,

Others but stewards of their excellence.

The summer's flower is to the summer sweet,

Though to itself it only live and die,

But if that flower with base infection meet,

The basest weed outbraves his dignity:

    For sweetest things turn sourest by their deeds;

    Lilies that fester smell far worse than weeds.

AS BETWEEN LILIES AND WEEDS

THESE WOULD SEEM TO BE the virtues of the upper class: not to hurt others just because they have the power to do so; not to abuse the attractiveness they possess in spades; though they stir the passions of others, to be themselves as steady as stone, inflexible, cold-blooded, resistant to temptation.

Land-owning aristocrats such as these rightly inherit heaven's graces, and guard nature's riches from waste. These are the lords and owners of their faces. Of such superiority lesser folk are but the servants.

In their aloofness the high-born are like a summer flower that sweetens its surroundings even though it lives and dies only to itself. But if that flower contracts a foul infection, the lowliest weed excels it. By their misdeeds, aristocrats turn the sweetest things into the sourest. For lilies that fester smell far worse than weeds.

Note: In this, often deemed the most puzzling of the *Sonnets*, the lowly poet seems to be warning his aristocratic friend that vices can turn the best into the worst. The last line is unique in being an exact quote from another source— the anonymous 1596 play *The Reign of King Edward III*. Does the poet hint here that he had a hand in that drama? / This is a rare sonnet: it contains neither *thou* nor *you*.

95

How sweet and lovely dost thou make the shame
Which, like a canker in the fragrant Rose,
Doth spot the beauty of thy budding name!
O! in what sweets dost thou thy sins enclose!
That tongue that tells the story of thy days,
Making lascivious comments on thy sport,
Cannot dispraise, but in a kind of praise;
Naming thy name blesses an ill report.
O! what a mansion have those vices got
Which for their habitation chose out thee,
Where beauty's veil doth cover every blot,
And all things turn to fair that eyes can see!
> *Take heed, dear heart, of this large privilege;*
> *The hardest knife ill-used doth lose his edge.*

YOUR CHARMS COVER
A MULTITUDE OF SINS

LIKE BLOTCHES ON a fragrant Rose, there are spots on the petals of your flowering reputation. But how sweet and lovely you make these embarrassments appear! With what honey do you coat your sins!

Tongues wag about how you spend your time; they make bawdy comments on your diversions. But even this disapproval seems a kind of praise. The citing of your name dignifies a nasty rumor.

What a hideaway those vices found when they chose you for their habitat. Your beauty veils every flaw and converts to charm your every outward aspect.

But beware, dear heart, of this generous privilege: abuse will dull the edge of even the sturdiest knife.

Note: L8: *Naming thy name*: the *Sonnets* was published in 1609; the *King James Bible* in 1611. In between, W.S. turned 46. In Psalm 46 of the *KJB*, the 46th word from the start is "shake"; the 46th from the end is "spear." (In the older *Geneva Bible*, the exact two words occur in almost the same relative location.) / There is no "spear" in the *Sonnets*, and only 9 in his entire writings; by contrast, "shake" occurs thrice in the *Sonnets* (including the outstanding S18 and S73), and 105 times over all.

96

Some say thy fault is youth, some wantonness;
    Some say thy grace is youth and gentle sport;
Both grace and faults are loved of more and less;
Thou mak'st faults graces that to thee resort.
As on the finger of a throned queen
The basest jewel will be well esteemed,
So are those errors that in thee are seen
To truths translated, and for true things deemed.
How many lambs might the stern wolf betray,
If like a lamb he could his looks translate!
How many gazers mightst thou lead away,
If thou wouldst use the strength of all thy state!
    But do not so; I love thee in such sort
    As thou being mine, mine is thy good report.

WHAT IS TRUE IN YOU, WHAT FALSE?

SOME PEOPLE SAY that your fault is youthfulness and wild behavior. Others say that your charm is youth and a gentleman's sporting life. But people of both the higher or lower classes love both your graces and your faults. You transform into graces those faults that attend you.

People will think highly of the cheapest jewel on the finger of a queen upon her throne. So what is false in you is twisted into truth and esteemed as genuine.

If the fierce wolf could look like a lamb, how many lambs would he trick! How many admirers you could lead astray if you exerted every power you possess!

But don't do it! You belong to me, and my love for you is such that your good reputation is mine as well.

Note: Queen Elizabeth had a "convert" Jewish doctor, Roderigo Lopez ("Wolf"). He had presented the Queen with a royal Spanish ring, which she did not accept until after he was hanged in 1594 for treason (perhaps unjustly). Some see him as the inspiration for W.S.'s Shylock. / Ls 13–14: something unique: the last two lines are identical with those ending another sonnet (S36); both wrap up a group of sonnets critical of the Youth.

97

How like a winter hath my absence been
From thee, the pleasure of the fleeting year!
What freezings have I felt, what dark days seen!
What old December's bareness everywhere!
And yet this time removed was summer's time,
The teeming autumn, big with rich increase,
Bearing the wanton burden of the prime,
Like widowed wombs after their lords' decease:
Yet this abundant issue seem'd to me
But hope of orphans and unfathered fruit;
For summer and his pleasures wait on thee,
And thou away, the very birds are mute;
Or, if they sing, 'tis with so dull a cheer,
That leaves look pale, dreading the winter's near.

IT MIGHT AS WELL
BE WINTER

IT MIGHT AS WELL be winter since I'm away from you—the one who gives the fleeting months their pleasure. What freezings have I felt, and dark days seen! What wizened December bareness gloomed on every side!

True, it was during this period of absence that the fruit of summer was born in a teeming autumn harvest, pregnant with abundance. Like a widow's womb after her husband's death, the fall carries summer's burden, sown in its lusty prime. Still, to me this fruitfulness seemed as forlorn as the hope of orphans, of fatherless children.

For the summer and its delights demand your presence, and when you are absent the very birds are mute. Or, if they sing, their charm is so dull that the leaves turn pale in dread of winter's nearness.

Note: L6: surprisingly, this is the only *big* in the *Sonnets*, which only twice have a *little*. / Back home in Stratford, the poet perhaps produced a sonnet or two like this one, which may have served as letters.

98

From you have I been absent in the spring,
When proud-pied April (dressed in all his
trim)
Hath put a spirit of youth in every thing,
That heavy Saturn laughed and leapt with him.
Yet nor the lays of birds, nor the sweet smell
Of different flowers in odour and in hue
Could make me any summer's story tell,
Or from their proud lap pluck them where they grew:
Nor did I wonder at the lily's white,
Nor praise the deep vermilion in the Rose;
They were but sweet, but figures of delight,
Drawn after you, you pattern of all those.
    Yet seemed it winter still, and, you away,
    As with your shadow I with these did play.

ONLY I HAD A
WINTRY APRIL

IT WAS SPRINGTIME when I left you. Dressed in all her splendid and various finery, April injected a youthful spirit into everything, and made even the ponderous planet Saturn laugh and skip.

Still, neither bird songs nor the sweetness of flowers in their various odors and colors could inspire me to invent a summer's tale, or even to pluck a blossom from the happy soil that bore it.

I didn't wonder at the whiteness of lilies, or praise the rich vermillion of the Rose. True, they were sweet enough, but nonetheless only parables of pleasure, modeled on you, the pattern of them all.

With you absent, the season seemed still to be winter, and I was merely toying with your shadows.

Note: L7: though surrounded by the glories of nature, the poet is absent from his friend, and so lacks the inspiration to compose a sunny play (like *A Midsummer Night's Dream*)—perhaps to counterbalance a sad *Winter's Tale.* / In the garden of the *Sonnets*, we encounter only one *garden*, and one *field*, but, along with 13 *Roses*, we cull 13 nameless *flowers*, three *lilies*, plus one *violet*, *marigold*, and *marjoram.* / L9: implies that the poet usually wonders at these simple wonders.

99

*T*he forward violet thus did I chide:
    "Sweet thief, whence didst thou steal thy sweet
        that smells,
If not from my love's breath? The purple pride
Which on thy soft cheek for complexion dwells
In my love's veins thou hast too grossly dyed."
The lily I condemned for thy hand,
And buds of marjoram had stol'n thy hair:
The Roses fearfully on thorns did stand,
One blushing shame, another white despair;
A third, nor red nor white, had stol'n of both,
And to his robbery had annexed thy breath,
But for his theft in pride of all his growth
A vengeful canker ate him up to death.
    More flowers I noted, yet I none could see
    But sweet or colour it had stol'n from thee.

FRAGRANCE AND HUE: STOLEN FROM YOU

THIS IS HOW I rebuked the presumptuous violet: Sweet thief, where did you steal your delicious odor, if not from my beloved's breath? It was from being too deeply dipped in my beloved's veins that you absorbed the purple splendor coloring your soft cheeks.

I condemned the lily for robbing paleness from your hands, and the knotted marjoram buds for filching fragrance from your hair.

Fearful Roses stood on their thorny stems— one, blushing red with shame, a second, white with despairing guilt, a third of neither color but stealing both, and breathing your breath as well. In punishment for such a thievery, a lethal worm was fatally eating this last one in its very prime.

I saw other flowers too, but I found none that had not purloined its fragrance and color from you.

Note: Uniquely, this sonnet has 15 lines. It details the last line of the previous sonnet, about playing with flowers. / The crimes: the violet stole one color and one fragrance; the lily stole only a color, and the marjoram only a fragrance. The red rose blushed from the shame of its thieving; the white rose paled from hopeless guilt; the pink rose stole both colors as well as the fragrance of the beloved's breath. For these three strikes, the pink rose was executed.

100

Where art thou, Muse, that thou forget'st
       so long
To speak of that which gives thee all thy might?
Spend'st thou thy fury on some worthless song,
Dark'ning thy power to lend base subjects light?
Return, forgetful Muse, and straight redeem
In gentle numbers time so idly spent;
Sing to the ear that doth thy lays esteem
And gives thy pen both skill and argument.
Rise, resty Muse, my love's sweet face survey,
If Time have any wrinkle graven there;
If any, be a Satire to decay,
And make Time's spoils despised everywhere.
    Give my love fame faster than Time wastes life;
    So thou prevent'st his scythe and crooked knife.

COME BACK, FORGETFUL MUSE!

WHERE HAVE YOU BEEN, my Muse, my poetic inspiration, that you have so long forgotten to sound the theme that gives you all your power?

Have you been squandering your awesome energy on some worthless song, darkening your gifts by shining their brightness on unworthy topics?

Come back, forgetful Muse, and with noble verses redeem at once the time you've wasted. Sing to my beloved, whose ear reveres your songs, and finds in them both skill and substance.

Rouse yourself, lazy Muse, and study my beloved's sweet face, to see if Time has carved any wrinkles there. If so, produce a satire on aging, and expose Time's ravages to universal scorn.

Give fame to my beloved faster than Time withers him. That way you will defeat the crooked blade of its sickle.

Note: The previous sonnet (99) can be seen as the end of a subordinate group, just as S126 concludes the whole group. Both S99 and S126 are odd: one has more lines than usual; the other, less. Is this oddness a signal?

101

O truant Muse, what shall be thy amends
　　For thy neglect of truth in beauty dyed?
Both truth and beauty on my love depends;
So dost thou too, and therein dignified.
Make answer, Muse: wilt thou not haply say
"Truth needs no colour, with his colour fixed;
Beauty no pencil, beauty's truth to lay;
But best is best, if never intermixed"?
Because he needs no praise, wilt thou be dumb?
Excuse not silence so; for't lies in thee
To make him much outlive a gilded tomb,
And to be praised of ages yet to be.
　　Then do thy office, Muse; I teach thee how
　　To make him seem long hence as he shows now.

NO MORE EXCUSE, MALINGERING MUSE!

YOU HOOKIE-PLAYING MUSE! How will you make up for your neglect of my ideal beloved, who is absolute Truth steeped in absolute Beauty? Truth and Beauty both depend on him; so do you, my Muse, and your dignity resides in lauding him.

How can you explain your silence? Will you perhaps argue that Truth needs no artistic coloring since its true colors are already firmly established? That beauty needs no brush to add layers to its splendor? That the best stays best when nothing is ever added to it? Will you remain dumb because my beloved needs no praise?

Please don't resort to excuses based so narrowly on the present moment! For it is within your power to preserve him much longer than any golden tomb could, and to make him praised by ages yet to come.

Do your job, Muse! I have reminded you how art can preserve for distant times the semblance of his present reality.

Note: L3: although as an artist W.S. would disagree with the philosopher Plato about the invalidity of art, he here agrees that earthly realities are mere flawed copies of Models/Forms which are perfect. Infatuated, the poet sees his friend as the Model for Truth, Beauty, and Goodness.

My love is strengthened, though more weak
    in seeming;
I love not less, though less the show appear:
That love is merchandized whose rich esteeming
The owner's tongue doth publish everywhere.
Our love was new and then but in the spring,
When I was wont to greet it with my lays;
As Philomel in summer's front doth sing,
And stops her pipe in growth of riper days:
Not that the summer is less pleasant now
Than when her mournful hymns did hush the night,
But that wild music burdens every bough,
And sweets grown common lose their dear delight.
    Therefore, like her, I sometime hold my tongue,
    Because I would not dull you with my song.

MORE CAN SEEM
LIKE LESS

MY LOVE FOR YOU has grown stronger, though
it may seem weaker. I love you no less, even though
I show it less. Love becomes a commodity when
the lover broadcasts all over the place how richly
he esteems the beloved.

When in the past I celebrated our love with
my poems, our feelings were new and in their
springtime. In the same way, the nightingale sings
at summer's start.

But she quiets her voice as the days grow shorter.
Her reason is not that the summer has grown less
pleasant since the time when her mournful tunes
first hushed the listening night.

No, her reason is that wild chirping now burdens
every bough, and when pleasures grow frequent they
lessen the delight that makes them dear.

Therefore, like the nightingale, I sometimes
hold my tongue. For I don't want to bore you with
my singing.

Note: L7: the mythical Philomel was changed into a nightingale after being
violated by her brother-in-law. Such classical references are rare in the
Sonnets. / L11: the wild chirping most likely stands for the clutch of rival poets
now seeking the rich Youth's patronage (and money).

103

A lack! what poverty my Muse brings forth,
 That, having such a scope to show her pride,
The argument all bare is of more worth
Than when it hath my added praise beside!
O blame me not if I no more can write!
Look in your glass, and there appears a face
That overgoes my blunt invention quite,
Dulling my lines, and doing me disgrace.
Were it not sinful, then, striving to mend,
To mar the subject that before was well?
For to no other pass my verses tend
Than of your graces and your gifts to tell;
   And more, much more, than in my verse can sit
   Your own glass shows you when you look in it.

A WRITER'S BLOCK EXPLAINED

ALAS, WHAT SHABBY results my Muse produces! She had such a chance to show her mettle. Yet the unvarnished subject was more praiseworthy before he received the additive of my would-be praise.

Please don't blame me if I can't write any more sonnets. Gaze into the mirror and see a face that surpasses my clumsy creativity, eclipses my verses, and occasions my disgrace.

Wouldn't it be a sin, then, to mar a perfect subject by trying to improve on it? Still, my writing had no other goal than to capture your gracious endowments.

When you look into that mirror, you will see very much more than could ever be reflected in my sonnets.

Note: Though W.S. uses the comparatively new word "mirror" a dozen times in his other works, he never uses it in the *Sonnets. Glass*, however, appears 10 times, 8 times as a looking glass. The word "mirror" comes from "mirus," the Latin word for "wonderful" (as in *mir*/acle); people naturally stare ad/*mir*/ingly at something wonderful (such as a *mir*/age). But, ironically, you can end up staring in a *mir*/ror even at a sight which is not so wonderful.

104

To me, fair friend, you never can be old,
   For as you were when first your eye I eyed,
Such seems your beauty still. Three winters cold
Have from the forests shook three summers' pride,
Three beauteous springs to yellow Autumn turned
In process of the seasons have I seen,
Three April perfumes in three hot Junes burned,
Since first I saw you fresh which yet are green.
Ah! yet doth beauty, like a dial hand,
Steal from his figure and no pace perceived;
So your sweet hue, which methinks still doth stand,
Hath motion, and mine eye may be deceived:
   For fear of which, hear this, thou age unbred:
   Ere you were born was beauty's summer dead.

THE FIRST TIME EVER I SAW YOUR FACE...

—EWAN MACCOLL

TO ME, FAIR FRIEND, you never can grow old. For just as you were when I first saw your eyes, just so seems your beauty still.

Even now you are as green as when I first gazed on your freshness. That, despite the fact that since then frigid winter has thrice stripped the forests of their summer glory. In the parade of the seasons I've seen three lovely springs turn to golden autumn, and April's perfumes thrice consumed by the heat of June.

But Ah! beauty creeps away from its peak of perfection like the hands of a clock—without seeming to move. So too is your sweet appearance subject to change. True, it seems to me to be motionless, but I could be wrong.

Fearing that I am wrong, I speak this message to ages as yet unconceived: before any of you were born, beauty's proudest summer had already come and gone.

Note: S104 is unique in citing a specific time span (three years) in W.S.'s bond with the Youth. It may not be literal; three was a favorite number with poets. / L2: *eye I eyed*: is this comical phrase the stutter of a besotted admirer? / S104 gives the only example of a mix of *you* and *thou*. S42 mixes *thou* and *ye*; S111, *you* and *ye*. In both cases *ye* is singular. For *thou* versus *you*, see S13.

105

Let not my love be called idolatry,
Nor my beloved as an idol show,
Since all alike my songs and praises be
To one, of one, still such, and ever so.
Kind is my love today, tomorrow kind,
Still constant in a wondrous excellence;
Therefore my verse, to constancy confined,
One thing expressing, leaves out difference.
"Fair, kind, and true" is all my argument,
"Fair, kind, and true," varying to other words.
And in this change is my invention spent,
Three themes in one, which wondrous scope affords.
*   "Fair, kind, and true," have often lived alone,*
*   Which three till now never kept seat in one.*

THE OLD REFRAIN

DON'T LET MY LOVE be called polytheistic, or my beloved seem to be one idol of many. For all my songs and praises are addressed to one person, concern one person, and still do, and always will.

My beloved is kind today, and will be so tomorrow, since he is "constant in a wondrous excellence." That's why my sonnets are forever focused on expressing a single theme, and omit everything else.

I want to argue that he is "lovely, kind, and true"; I say "lovely, kind, and true" in as many ways as I can. Finding amazing fertility in this three-in-one theme, I devote all my creativity to rhapsodizing about it.

Loveliness, kindness, and truthfulness have often individually adorned this person or that. But until you, they were never enthroned in the same single person.

Note: In this, the first of several divinizing sonnets, W.S. boldly borrows familiar prayer formulas, and stresses three, to make his beloved a kind of Trinity. (The poet's lifelong parish church at Stratford was named Holy Trinity in honor of God the Father, the Son, and the Holy Ghost.) / Ls 9, 10, 13: *fair, kind, and true* correspond to the basic triad of Beauty, Goodness, and Truth.

When in the chronicle of wasted time
  I see descriptions of the fairest wights,
And beauty making beautiful old rhyme
In praise of ladies dead and lovely knights,
Then, in the blazon of sweet beauty's best,
Of hand, of foot, of lip, of eye, of brow,
I see their antique pen would have expressed
Even such a beauty as you master now.
So all their praises are but prophecies
Of this our time, all you prefiguring;
And for they looked but with divining eyes,
They had not skill enough your worth to sing:
   For we, which now behold these present days,
   Have eyes to wonder, but lack tongues to praise.

LADIES DEAD AND LOVELY KNIGHTS

AT TIMES, in the annals of bygone days, I read descriptions of wonderfully winsome souls, and find human beauty inspiring beautiful old rhymes written in praise of "ladies dead and lovely knights."

As these rhymes describe the best features of sweet beauty—the charming hand and foot and lip and eye and brow—I see that these antique pens wanted to express beauty of the sort now incarnated in you.

So all their praises are but prophecies of the present, and prefigure you entirely. But since they foresaw with the eye of distant divination, they lacked sufficient clarity to celebrate your excellence worthily.

Even we who live in this time of fulfillment and who have the eyes to be astonished, still lack the tongues to utter proper praise.

Note: More divinization: Christian writers saw many *Old Testament* personages and events as prefiguring Christ. The poet sees many ancient poems as prefiguring his beloved. / L2: *wight*: creature/person. / L4: *lovely* is an interesting word applied here to knights instead of ladies. / L5: *blazon*: description, as of a coat of arms.

107

ot mine own fears, nor the prophetic soul
Of the wide world dreaming on things
to come,

Can yet the lease of my true love control,

Supposed as forfeit to a confined doom.

The mortal moon hath her eclipse endured

And the sad augurs mock their own presage;

Incertainties now crown themselves assured,

And peace proclaims olives of endless age.

Now with the drops of this most balmy time

My love looks fresh, and Death to me subscribes,

Since, spite of him, I'll live in this poor rhyme,

While he insults o'er dull and speechless tribes:

    And thou in this shalt find thy monument,

    When tyrants' crests and tombs of brass are spent.

MY POEMS WILL PRESERVE US BOTH

NEITHER MY OWN DREAD, nor prophetic spirits everywhere—dreaming of what was to come—could correctly predict the end of my true love's life, supposedly condemned to a prison death.

Our mortal moon, the Queen, has suffered her final eclipse, and the doom-mongers now mock their own predictions. What was uncertain is now crowned with surety, and our time of peace promises to bear its olives forever.

The coronation oils have proven a powerful balm to the times. My beloved looks refreshed and even death yields to me. For, in spite of mortality, I'll survive in this fragile poetry while death insolently obliterates people who are mindless and mute.

You too will find your monument in these pages, while the coats of arms of tyrants fade, and their brassy tombs collapse.

Note: L11: a new twist: these poems will immortalize the poet too. (S125 may imply that W.S. later gave up on the whole idea of immortality through poetry.) / S107 seems to reflect the nervous times in England from the death of Elizabeth in 1603 to the accession of King James I. / If L13's *you* is H.W., then S107 may be celebrating the full pardon he received from the new King. Elizabeth had already commuted his death sentence for treason to life imprisonment. The treason consisted in his backing the Earl of Essex in his 1601 rebellion against the Queen.

108

*W*hat's in the brain that ink may character
    Which hath not figured to thee my true
  spirit?
What's new to speak, what now to register,
That may express my love, or thy dear merit?
Nothing, sweet boy; but yet, like prayers divine,
I must, each day say o'er the very same,
Counting no old thing old, thou mine, I thine,
Even as when first I hallow'd thy fair name.
So that eternal love in love's fresh case
Weighs not the dust and injury of age,
Nor gives to necessary wrinkles place,
But makes antiquity for aye his page;
    Finding the first conceit of love there bred,
    Where time and outward form would show it
dead.

THE FUNDAMENTAL THINGS OF LIFE, AS TIME GOES BY
—HERMAN HUPFELD

WHAT IS LEFT in my brain, capable of being verbalized, which hasn't already been used to spell out for you my honest feelings? What is new for the speaking, or fresh for the recording, that can express either my love for you, or your own precious worth?

Nothing, "sweet boy." Yet, like daily prayers, I must repeat the same words every day. You are mine; I am yours: these old phrases I do not consider old, any more than I did when I first blessed your lovely name.

Thus I am proving that undying love, in each fresh embodiment, pays no attention to the debris and damage of increasing age. Nor does it retreat in the face of inevitable wrinkles. Rather, such love makes "forever" the endless theme of its pages.

This is true, even though the oldest expressions of love were first formulated in volumes whose age and outward look would suggest dead ideas.

Note: More divinization: the poet prays, "Hallowed be thy name" (*Matthew* 6:9). / L5: *sweet boy*: though H.W. could have been in his twenties, W.H. would have been seven years younger than H.W. / L7: one of W.S.'s ideals is mutuality in love—a balanced give-and-take. In the *Sonnets*, *mine* occurs 63 times; *thine*, 44 times; *myself*, 29 times; *thyself*, 21 times.

109

O! never say that I was false of heart,
Though absence seem'd my flame to qualify;
As easy might I from myself depart
As from my soul, which in thy breast doth lie:
That is my home of love: if I have ranged,
Like him that travels, I return again;
Just to the time, not with the time exchanged,
So that myself bring water for my stain.
Never believe, though in my nature reign'd
All frailties that besiege all kinds of blood,
That it could so preposterously be stained,
To leave for nothing all thy sum of good;
   For nothing this wide universe I call,
   Save thou, my Rose; in it thou art my all.

THE PRODIGAL SONNETEER RETURNS

DON'T EVER SAY my heart was false, even though my absence seemed to diminish its flame. I might as easily take leave of myself as abandon that soul of mine which dwells in your breast. There is my home of love.

If I have ranged, I return again like a traveler— right on time, but not changed by time. By my very returning I wash away the stain of having left.

Even if every weakness that infects every kind of passion ruled in my nature, never believe that my nature could be so outrageously tainted that I could abandon for some nobody all the goodness of you.

For I count this wide universe itself as a nothing—except for you, my Rose. You are everything that the universe means to me.

Note: Divinization again: the beloved is equated with supreme value. / L14: for *Rose*, see S1. The poet was a visitor to H.W.'s main country seat, at Titchfield, which contained roses in its heraldic decorations. / L14: *thou, my Rose*: it was a woman who was usually called a rose by a man, but the poet may have had a special meaning in mind. The very third line of the first poem which W.S. dedicated to H.W. begins with "Rose-cheeked Adonis."

110

Alas! 'tis true, I have gone here and there,
And made myself a motley to the view,
Gored mine own thoughts, sold cheap what is most
    dear,
Made old offences of affections new.
Most true it is that I have looked on truth
Askance and strangely: but, by all above,
These blenches gave my heart another youth,
And worse essays proved thee my best of love.
Now all is done, have what shall have no end:
Mine appetite I never more will grind
On newer proof, to try an older friend,
A god in love, to whom I am confined.
   Then give me welcome, next my heaven the best,
   Even to thy pure and most most loving breast.

ABSENCE MADE MY HEART GROW FONDER

SORRY, BUT IT'S TRUE that I have gone a-roving, made a public fool of myself, violated my own ideals, sold on the cheap what is most precious, and abused old bonds by forging new ones.

It's quite true that I have looked askance at my true situation, as though it were something unfamiliar.

But I swear by all the heavens that these spells of withdrawal rejuvenated my heart. By trying something worse I have proven you to be my best love. All that is over now, except what shall never have an end.

Never again will I hone my appetite on someone new as a way of testing an older friend, one who is a god in loving, and to whom I am exclusively committed.

Then, welcome me back, you who are the next best thing to heaven. Welcome me to your pure, supremely loving breast.

Note: This sonnet seems to contradict its predecessor, but it still divinizes *a god in love, next my heaven the best.* / L2: recalling the pied costume of jesters, *I have... made myself a motley to the view* may refer to the poet's acting as a clown on the stage and/or in real life. / L7: *blenches*: withdrawals. / L14: *most most*: a super-superlative.

111

O! for my sake do you with Fortune chide,
The guilty goddess of my harmful deeds,
That did not better for my life provide
Than public means which public manners breeds.
Thence comes it that my name receives a brand,
And almost thence my nature is subdued
To what it works in, like the dyer's hand.
Pity me then and wish I were renewed,
Whilst, like a willing patient, I will drink
Potions of eisel 'gainst my strong infection;
No bitterness that I will bitter think,
Nor double penance, to correct correction.
    Pity me then, dear friend, and I assure ye
    Even that your pity is enough to cure me.

OCCUPATIONAL STIGMA

PLEASE, DEAR FRIEND, argue with Fate on my behalf. She's the guilty goddess responsible for my offensive behavior. She's the one who failed to provide me with a livelihood in some better field than the public life which breeds vulgar manners.

Thus it happens that my name is stigmatized, with my identity almost reduced to my occupation. I am stained by my work, like a dyer's hand.

Pity me then, and wish for my rehabilitation. In the meantime, like a cooperative patient, I will quaff down vinegary potions to fight my bad infection. To correct what needs correcting, I will judge no bitterness too bitter, nor will I object to even a double curing dose.

Pity me, then, for I assure you that your pity alone is enough to heal me… without the vinegar.

Note: L10: *eisel*: vinegar. / In W.S.'s day, "Life upon the wicked stage" (alias "Satan's Chapel") was regarded by Puritans and others as sinful. Women were not allowed to act, and London's theaters had to be outside the city. Nor were plays regarded as literature; the best printers did not bother with them. Indeed, in the dedication of the *First Folio* of 36 of W.S.'s plays, even the editors, once his fellow actors, thrice refer to these priceless masterpieces as "trifles."

112

*Y*our love and pity doth th'impression fill
    Which vulgar scandal stamped upon my
brow,

For what care I who calls me well or ill,

So you o'er-green my bad, my good allow?

You are my all-the-world, and I must strive

To know my shames and praises from your tongue;

None else to me, nor I to none alive,

That my steeled sense o'er-changes right or wrong.

In so profound Abyss I throw all care

Of others' voices, that my adder's sense

To critic and to flatterer stopped are.

Mark how with my neglect I do dispense:

    You are so strongly in my purpose bred

    That all the world besides methinks y'are dead.

YOU ALONE TEACH ME RIGHT AND WRONG

YOUR LOVE AND YOUR PITY repair the wound with which vulgar scandal has branded my brow. For what do I care who calls me good or bad, so long as you gloss over my bad and confirm my good?

You are the whole world to me, and I must try to learn from your lips alone what my shames and merits are. Since I regard only you as truly alive (as do you me), you alone can modify my rooted sense of right and wrong.

Into such a deep canyon do I chuck all concern for the opinion of others, that my ears (deaf as a snake's) are shut to critic and flatterer alike.

See how I implement my intention to ignore: you are so strongly embedded in what I care about that in my view everyone else has ceased to exist.

Note: Further divinized, the Youth now becomes the sole judge of good and evil. / L4: in its original spelling, *o'er-greene* may be a play on the name of Robert Greene (cf. S70), who made the first public attack on W.S. the dramatist. Greene called him an "upstart crow." (A crow waits in the wings of the next sonnet.) / L8: *my steeled sense o'er-changes right or wrong*: an obscure line. / L10: the adder was reputed to be able to deafen itself at will.

Since I left you, mine eye is in my mind;
    And that which governs me to go about
Doth part his function and is partly blind,
Seems seeing, but effectually is out;
For it no form delivers to the heart
Of bird, of flower, or shape, which it doth latch;
Of his quick objects hath the mind no part;
Nor his own vision holds what it doth catch:
For if it see the rud'st or gentlest sight,
The most sweet-favoured or deformed'st creature,
The mountain, or the sea, the day, or night,
The crow or dove, it shapes them to your feature.
    Incapable of more, replete with you,
    My most true mind thus makes mine eye untrue.

I ONLY HAVE EYES FOR YOU

—AL DUBIN

SINCE I LEFT YOU, my eye is in my mind. The bodily sense that shows me where to go isn't completely working, is partly blind. It appears to be seeing, but is practically extinguished.

For my eye delivers to my heart no form of bird or flower, or any other shape it focuses on. My mind registers no living object that the eye can see. Indeed, even the eye cannot retain its catch.

My eye makes everything assume your shape: the rudest or the gentlest sight, creatures the most favored or deformed, the mountain or sea, day or night, crow or dove.

Filled to the brim, saturated with you, the truest vision of my mind falsifies my outward vision.

Note: How miraculously attentive and retentive must have been young W.S.'s eyes as they absorbed the graces of the golden heart of Britain. Near the Forest of Arden and the flowering meadows of south central England, his native village of Stratford lay in a richly agricultural area. Mentioned in a 692 A.D. document, its name referred to a "straight" Roman road which crossed a ford in the River Avon (from the Welsh word for "river"). In the preface to the *First Folio* of 1623, fellow playwright Ben Jonson was the first to call "gentle Shakespeare" "the sweet Swan of Avon," as well as "the Soul of the Age," who was "not of an age, but for all time." See S117.

114

*O*r whether doth my mind, being crowned
  with you,

Drink up the monarch's plague, this flattery?

Or whether shall I say, mine eye saith true,

And that your love taught it this Alchemy,

To make of monsters and things indigest

Such cherubins as your sweet self resemble,

Creating every bad a perfect best,

As fast as objects to his beams assemble?

O! 'tis the first, 'tis flatt'ry in my seeing,

And my great mind most kingly drinks it up;

Mine eye well knows what with his gust is 'greeing,

And to his palate doth prepare the cup.

  If it be poisoned, 'tis the lesser sin

  That mine eye loves it and doth first begin.

MY EYE CONDITION: FLATTERY OR ALCHEMY?

HOW EXPLAIN THE WAY my eye sees you (smiling at me) everywhere? Made a king by your love, does my mind drink up impressions produced by the kind of flattery that is the curse of kings?

Or does my eye see truly? Has your love taught it this alchemy—to turn monsters and crudities into cherubs which resemble your sweet self, making everything bad a perfect best as soon it comes into focus before me?

I'm afraid it's the first case—my eye flatters, and my lordly mind drinks up the flattery like a king. My eye knows well what pleases my mind's palate, and so prepares the cup to suit it.

If the cup turns out to be poisoned, the eye's guilt will be less, since the eye too loves the potion, and tests it first, like a royal taster.

Note: L11: *with his gust is 'greeing*: agreeable to his palate (gustatory organ).

115

Those lines that I before have writ do lie,
Even those that said I could not love you
dearer;
Yet then my judgement knew no reason why
My most full flame should afterwards burn clearer.
But reckoning Time, whose millioned accidents
Creep in 'twixt vows and change decrees of kings,
Tan sacred beauty, blunt the sharp'st intents,
Divert strong minds to the course of altering things;
Alas! why, fearing of Time's tyranny,
Might I not then say, "Now I love you best,"
When I was certain o'er incertainty,
Crowning the present, doubting of the rest?
    Love is a babe; then might I not say so,
    To give full growth to that which still doth grow?

ERRATUM: MY LOVE *HAS* GROWN

THOSE VERSES I wrote earlier are mistaken—the ones which said I couldn't love you any more than I did. But at the time, my imagination could not conceive how the full intensity of my love would blaze even more brightly at a later date.

Even then I realized how time and its million accidents creep in between vows, alter the decrees of kings, discolor sacred beauty, blunt the sharpest intentions, and divert fixed minds into following the currents of change.

So, fearing time's tyranny, why mightn't I have honestly said, "Now I love you most intensely"? After all, at that moment I was certain beyond a doubt, eager to crown the moment at hand, and unsure of any future.

New love is a baby. Was I then not justified in saying what I did so that I might promote the full growth of what was still growing?

Note: There is an opposite way to read the last two lines: "Love is a growth-oriented baby, so I should not have claimed what I did—attributing maturity to what was still growing."

116

*L*et me not to the marriage of true minds
　Admit impediments. Love is not love
Which alters when it alteration finds,
Or bends with the remover to remove.
O no! it is an ever-fixed mark
That looks on tempests and is never shaken;
It is the star to every wand'ring bark,
Whose worth's unknown, although his height be
　　taken.
Love's not Time's fool, though rosy lips and cheeks
Within his bending sickle's compass come;
Love alters not with his brief hours and weeks,
But bears it out even to the edge of doom.
　If this be error and upon me proved,
　I never writ, nor no man ever loved.

TRUE LOVE IS NOT THE FOOL OF TIME

YOU WON'T FIND ME agreeing that the commitment of a genuine lover can ever be annulled. Love is not true love if it changes when it encounters change, or deviates in response to a partner's distancing.

Not at all! It is an immovable lighthouse that looks on tempests but is never shaken. It is a star for all wandering ships—a star whose mystery remains though some of its aspects be measured.

"Love is not Time's fool," though rosy lips and cheeks fall within the sweep of Time's curved sickle. Love does not pass away with the swift passage of Time's hours and weeks. Rather, it endures till the very edge of doom.

If anyone can prove to me that all this is wrong, then I never wrote a word, nor has any man ever truly loved.

Note: It has long been thought that this is merely a definition sonnet ("What is love?"). But scholar Helen Vendler sees the marvelous S116 as a refutation sonnet. The tip-off is the accent on the second word of the sonnet: let ME not. She argues that the poet's young friend had questioned the constancy of love (W.S.'s or anyone's), and W.S. is here counter-arguing. See S49.

117

A ccuse me thus: that I have scanted all
    Wherein I should your great deserts repay,
Forgot upon your dearest love to call,
Whereto all bonds do tie me day by day;
That I have frequent been with unknown minds,
And given to time your own dear-purchased right;
That I have hoisted sail to all the winds
Which should transport me farthest from your sight.
Book both my wilfulness and errors down,
And on just proof surmise accumulate;
Bring me within the level of your frown,
But shoot not at me in your wakened hate;
   Since my appeal says I did strive to prove
   The constancy and virtue of your love.

THIS WAS ONLY A TEST

LET THIS BE your accusation: that I have neglected all the ways in which I should repay your great deserving; that I have forgotten to invoke your most precious love (though every bond links me to it day by day), that I have often spent time with mere acquaintances and devoted to them the hours which by costly purchase rightly belong to you, and that I have hoisted my sail to all the winds that might take me farthest from your sight.

Make a list of all my wanderings and mistakes, and estimate the accumulated total on the basis of what has already been proven. Bring me within the target of your frown, but do not shoot at me out of your stirred-up anger.

For my excuse is that I was testing the persistence and perfection of your love.

Note: About 75 miles northwest of London, the town of Stratford-upon-Avon is now inextricably linked to one of its 16th-century natives. His father, however, was born in Snitterfield, four miles to the north; his mother at Wilmcote, three miles to the north; his wife at Shottery, one mile to the west. The town of his marriage was probably Temple Grafton, five miles to the west.

118

*L*ike as, to make our appetites more keen,
  With eager compounds we our palate urge,
As to prevent our maladies unseen,
We sicken to shun sickness when we purge:
Even so, being full of your ne'er-cloying sweetness,
To bitter sauces did I frame my feeding;
And, sick of welfare, found a kind of meetness
To be diseased, ere that there was true needing.
Thus policy in love, to anticipate
The ills that were not, grew to faults assur'd,
And brought to medicine a healthful state,
Which, rank of goodness, would by ill be cured.
    But thence I learn, and find the lesson true,
    Drugs poison him that so fell sick of you.

RATIONALIZING UNFAITHFULNESS

SOMETIMES, TO SHARPEN our appetite, we stimulate our palates with bitter-tasting concoctions. Or, on occasion, we actually sicken ourselves with purges to head off potential maladies.

Just so, being full of your never-filling sweetness, I added bitter sauces to my diet. Tired of being well, I thought it appropriate to make myself sick even before there was need to do so.

This clever plan of mine, anticipating ills that had not yet befallen, led to definite ailments and induced me to medicate my healthy state. My hope was that, overdosed with goodness, my condition might be cured by ill.

But I learned a lesson from all of this: medicines poison the lover who falls sick of you the way I did.

Note: L2: eager: at one time the adjective meant sharp or sour (e.g., "vin/egar," that is, sharp wine).

119

*What potions have I drunk of **Siren** tears,*
    Distilled from limbecks foul as hell within,
Applying fears to hopes, and hopes to fears,
Still losing when I saw myself to win!
What wretched errors hath my heart committed,
Whilst it hath thought itself so blessed never!
How have mine eyes out of their spheres been fitted
In the distraction of this madding fever!
O benefit of ill! now I find true
That better is by evil still made better;
And ruin'd love, when it is built anew,
Grows fairer than at first, more strong, far greater.
    So I return rebuked to my content,
    And gain by ill thrice more than I have spent.

LOVE IS BETTER THE SECOND TIME AROUND

—SAMMY CAHN

WHAT DRAFTS HAVE I drunk of enchanting liquors brewed in beakers as foul as hell! Keeping me a loser when I saw myself winning at last, these potions made my fears hopeful, and my hopes fearful.

What dreadful mistakes my heart committed just when it thought it had never felt so happy! In the distress of this mad fever, how my eyes have rolled around in dislocating fits!

Still, what benefits have flowed from all this evil! Now I find it true that what is better can be made better yet by bouts with evil. When collapsed love is rebuilt it becomes lovelier than it was, stronger, far greater.

So I come back to myself, happy in having been rebuffed. From bad times I've gained three times more profit than I ever wasted.

Note: L1: *Siren*: bewitching mermaid. / L2: *limbecks*: glass vessels used for laboratory distillations. / L4: *still*: always.

120

*T*hat you were once unkind befriends me now,
  And for that sorrow which I then did feel
Needs must I under my transgression bow,
Unless my nerves were brass or hammered steel.
For if you were by my unkindness shaken
As I by yours, you've passed a hell of time,
And I, a tyrant, have no leisure taken
To weigh how once I suffered in your crime.
O, that our night of woe might have remembered
My deepest sense, how hard true sorrow hits,
And soon to you, as you to me, then tendered
The humble salve which wounded bosoms fits!
    But that your trespass now becomes a fee;
    Mine ransoms yours, and yours must ransom me.

ONE HELL OF A TIME

THAT YOU WERE ONCE unkind to me is now a comfort. As I remember how cruelty hurts, I realize that I should surrender to my awareness of what my transgression has now done to you. After all, my conscience is not made of brass or hammered steel.

For if you have been as shaken by my unkindness as I was by yours, you've been through hell. Meanwhile, like a heartless tyrant, I have not paused to recall what the suffering was like which I endured at your harming hands.

Would that our night of grief had activated my keen realization of how terrible genuine regret makes the offender feel. Then I would have immediately applied to you, as you did to me, the ointment of apology that soothes a wounded heart.

I now regard your old offense a debt. My mercy canceled yours; yours must now cancel mine.

Note: H.W. was financially kind after W.S. dedicated to him his first poem. (See S75.) The poet had vowed "to take advantage of all idle hours, till I have honoured you with some graver labour." The latter was *The Rape of Lucrece* (1594), whose 97-word dedication begins: "The love I dedicate to your lordship is without end... The warrant I have of your honourable disposition, not the worth of my untutored lines, makes it assured of acceptance." (See S26.)

'Tis better to be vile than vile esteemed,
  When not to be receives reproach of being,
And the just pleasure lost, which is so deemed
Not by our feeling but by others' seeing.
For why should others' false adulterate eyes
Give salutation to my sportive blood?
Or on my frailties why are frailer spies,
Which in their wills count bad what I think good?
No, I am that I am, and they that level
At my abuses reckon up their own;
I may be straight, though they themselves be bevel;
By their rank thoughts my deeds must not be shown,
    Unless this general evil they maintain,
    All men are bad, and in their badness reign.

HYPOCRITES OR MISANTHROPES?

IT IS BETTER to be corrupt than to be thought corrupt, when what isn't foul is condemned for being so, and the just pleasure of a good reputation is thereby lost. I don't mean lost in one's own conscience, but in the opinion of others.

For why should the false, adulterous eyes of others wink a knowing wink at my presumed lust? Why do people who are even less self-disciplined than I am spy on my weaknesses, people who judge things evil which I regard as good?

No, I am what I am, and those who focus on my supposed abuses multiply their own. It may be that I am straight, while they themselves are crooked. My deeds must not be measured by their filthy minds.

Unless, of course, they believe in universal evil, and maintain that all men are bad, and evil always wins.

Note: Is W.S. reacting to base interpretations of his love for his young friend? / L9: in *Exodus* 3:14, "God said unto Moses, 'I AM THAT I AM.'" Surely the poet knew that many would find this self-applied borrowing blasphemous.

*T*hy gift, thy tables, are within my brain
  Full charactered with lasting memory,
Which shall above that idle rank remain
Beyond all date, even to eternity;
Or, at the least, so long as brain and heart
Have faculty by nature to subsist;
Till each to razed oblivion yield his part
Of thee, thy record never can be missed.
That poor retention could not so much hold,
Nor need I tallies thy dear love to score;
Therefore to give them from me was I bold,
To trust those tables that receive thee more:
    To keep an adjunct to remember thee
    Were to import forgetfulness in me.

MY MEMORY OF YOU IS THE SAFEST JOURNAL

MY SONNETS, transcribed in the journal that you gave to me, are fully inscribed in my brain for everlasting memory. There they will outlive mere sheets of lifeless pages. There they will survive for all time, even to eternity—or at least as long as nature grants survival to brain and heart.

The memory of you can never be lost until brain and heart have been crushed into oblivion, and surrender those parts of you they captured.

Sketchy journals could not retain that much, nor do I need some scoreboard to tally up the measure of your dear love. Therefore, trusting rather in those inner pages that embrace more of you, I dared to give the journals away.

If I needed to hold on to some other aid for remembering you, I would be admitting that I could forget you.

Note: In the Bard's day, a sheet of paper could cost as much as a loaf of bread. / L4: like the opening words of the dedication (*Eternity, Ever-living*), the *Sonnets* focus on "forever"—though that precise word never shows up. What do appear are *ever/e'er* (23), *eternal* (6), *eternity* (4), *evermore* (3), *dateless*, and *perpetual* (2). Single instances occur for *always, aye, boundless, endless, ever-living,* and *immortal.* "Everlasting," "immortality," "infinite," and "infinity" do not appear.

123

*N*o, Time, thou shalt not boast that I do
    change:
Thy pyramids built up with newer might
To me are nothing novel, nothing strange;
They are but dressings of a former sight.
Our dates are brief, and therefore we admire
What thou dost foist upon us that is old,
And rather make them born to our desire
Than think that we before have heard them told.
Thy registers and thee I both defy,
Not wondering at the present, nor the past,
For thy records and what we see doth lie,
Made more or less by thy continual haste.
    This I do vow and this shall ever be:
    I will be true, despite thy scythe and thee.

OLD NOVELTIES

NO YOU DON'T, TIME! You will never be able to brag that you have changed me. For I am already sure that not everything is new.

[As we both know, here in London] "pyramids" were recently built [for King James's welcoming ceremonies]. Though they represented the latest technology, to me these structures were not at all new or exotic. They were just updated versions of previous designs.

Our lifespans are short, and therefore, [Sir] Time, people are impressed by the antiquities you palm off on us as something fresh. Besides, we would rather see these things as creations of our own desires than think that we have heard tell of them before.

But, Time, I defy both you and your record books. I refuse to be impressed by either your current achievements or your past ones. For the records of your past, as well as those which our own eyes behold, are deceptive. Your incessant haste makes things seem either more or less than they are.

But this is my eternal vow, and this will never change: I will be faithful in love, despite you and your obliterating scythe.

Note: Another "most difficult sonnet" contestant. For that reason, I've paraphrased somewhat more freely than usual.

*I*f my dear love were but the child of state,
   It might for Fortune's bastard be unfathered,
As subject to Time's love, or to Time's hate,
Weeds among weeds, or flowers with flowers gathered.
No, it was builded far from accident;
It suffers not in smiling pomp, nor falls
Under the blow of thralled discontent,
Whereto the inviting time our fashion calls;
It fears not Policy, that heretic,
Which works on leases of short-numbered hours,
But all alone stands hugely politic,
That it nor grows with heat, nor drowns with
      showers.
   To this I witness call the fools of Time,
   Which die for goodness, who have lived for crime.

PASSION FREE
FROM FASHION

IF MY TENDER LOVE for you were conceived out
of political advantage, it could lose its paternity, and
by a twist of Fate become a bastard. For it would
be subject to fashionable approval or fashionable
rejection, now a weed among weeds, now a blossom
plucked up along with other blossoms.

But no; my love for you was begotten far from
the accidents of the times. It does not suffer secretly
under the mask of smiling ceremony; it does not
collapse under the threat of the prisons which await
malcontents. To such alternatives does the fashion of
current opportunities expose us.

Nor need my love for you fear love's heretic,
government cunning, which operates on short-
term leases. My love stands on its own two feet,
unsubsidized. It does not bloom under the warmth
of patronage, nor drown in its downpours. To the
wisdom of my cunning I summon as witnesses
"the fools of time"—those who criminally wasted
their lives, but then wisely choose to die repentant.

Note: The difficult S124 reminds us that W.S. lived in a time of religious and
political upheaval. / L6: this is the sole *smile* in *Shakespeare's Sonnets*, which
also contains a solitary *laugh* (S97) but five *frowns*.

125

W'ere't aught to me I bore the canopy,
 With my extern the outward honouring,
Or laid great bases for eternity,
Which prove more short than waste or ruining?
Have I not seen dwellers on form and favour
Lose all, and more, by paying too much rent,
For compound sweet forgoing simple savour,
Pitiful thrivers, in their gazing spent?
No, let me be obsequious in thy heart,
And take thou my oblation, poor but free,
Which is not mixed with seconds, knows no art
But mutual render, only me for thee.

   Hence, thou suborned informer! a true soul
   When most impeached stands least in thy control.

'TIS THE GIFT TO BE SIMPLE

—Joseph Brackett

DON'T SUPPOSE THAT it meant all that much to me that I carried a processional canopy, and endorsed outward show with my outward behavior. Or that it was for my own eternal fame that I worked to build, by means of my sonnets, foundations which I now see have a life briefer than any structure which is now wasted or ruined.

Have I not seen people who fawned on style and patronage lose everything by paying too high a price, by replacing simple pleasures with rich sweets? Their climb up the ladder was pitiful, as they consumed themselves with worshipful gazing.

Rather, let me be the servant of your inner worth. Accept my holy offering, plain but spontaneous. It is not cheapened by the second-rate. It knows no cleverness, but involves mutual surrender, where the only gift I give is myself.

Begone, then, you hired informer, critic of my sincerity! An honest man, when most accused, stands least under the sway of the likes of you.

Note: W.S. likely took part in ceremonies honoring King James I, the patron of his troupe. A spy claimed that W.S. sought selfish gain from his devotion to his prestigious friend.

O thou my lovely boy, who in thy power
　　 Dost hold Time's fickle glass, his sickle hour;
Who hast by waning grown, and therein show'st
Thy lover's withering, as thy sweet self grow'st;
If Nature, sovereign mistress over wrack,
As thou goest onwards, still will pluck thee back,
She keeps thee to this purpose, that her skill
May Time disgrace, and wretched minutes kill.
Yet fear her, O thou minion of her pleasure!
She may detain, but not still keep, her treasure:
　　 Her **Audit**, *though delayed, answered must be,*
　　 And her **Quietus** *is to render thee.*

NATURE CAN'T DELAY FOREVER

OH LOVELY BOY OF MINE! In your vigor you retard the sands of Time's hourglass, and delay its sickle's lethal hour. With the passing of Time you have matured. While I, your lover, was withering, your sweet self grew even sweeter.

If Nature, the sovereign mistress of all that decays, preserves your youth as you age, she does so for this purpose: that her skill may embarrass Time and kill off some of its murderous minutes.

Yet you should still fear Nature, though you are her pleasuring sweetheart. She can make her treasures loiter, but cannot hold them back forever. Though she delays meeting her debt, she must eventually pay it. To discharge her obligation she must discharge you as well.

Note: Like a coda ending the 125 "Fair Youth" series, this poem is unique: it is not a sonnet, but six rhyming couplets of the sort that normally conclude a sonnet. Is this an emphatic sixfold finale? / In the original edition, the usual final couplet is replaced by two sets of empty, widely-spaced parentheses. Various meanings have been read into this oddity: an hourglass, moons, love handles, the still empty final lines of time's account book for the poet and the Youth, two open graves. (See S77: "[Thy] wrinkles…Of mouthed graves will give thee memory.") / L1: some say (improbably, I say) that the lovely boy is the son of W.H., whose birth would neatly close the circle of these sonnets.

127

In the old age black was not counted fair,
  Or if it were, it bore not beauty's name;
But now is black beauty's successive heir,
And beauty slandered with a bastard shame:
For since each hand hath put on Nature's power,
Fairing the foul with Art's false borrowed face,
Sweet beauty hath no name, no holy bower,
But is profaned, if not lives in disgrace.
Therefore my mistress' eyes are raven black,
Her eyes so suited, and they mourners seem
At such who, not born fair, no beauty lack,
Sland'ring creation with a false esteem:
  Yet so they mourn, becoming of their woe,
  That every tongue says beauty should look so.

FAIR IS FOUL, AND FOUL IS FAIR

—*MACBETH* (1.1.11–12)

IN FORMER TIMES, a dark complexion was not considered lovely—or if it was, not fair enough to be deemed truly beautiful. But nowadays "black is beautiful." Old-fashioned fairness is now slandered with the shame of illegitimacy.

How so? Because today, thanks to cosmetics, every woman's hand can ape nature's power, and beautify the ugly with a complexion fair but phony. The result is that trueborn fairness is no longer in repute. It has no sacred shrine, is mocked, if not actually banished in disgrace.

So, following fashion, I've chosen a mistress whose curls are as black as ravens, with eyes to match. Those eyes seem to be grieving that those women who, though born without beauty, are now absolutely gorgeous. Those eyes mourn that the natural is being defamed by the artificial.

Yet, as befits my lady's woe, her dark eyes lament in such a beguiling way that everybody swears that she is the very standard of beauty.

Note: After 126 mainly man-to-man poems, here begin 28 sonnets chiefly involving *a woman colored ill*—notably contrasted with *a man right fair.* (See S144.) / L9: the poet here bluntly admits (to whom, though?) that he has taken a mistress.

How oft, when thou, my music, music play'st,
Upon that blessed wood whose motion sounds
With thy sweet fingers, when thou gently sway'st
The wiry concord that mine ear confounds,
Do I envy those jacks that nimble leap
To kiss the tender inward of thy hand,
Whilst my poor lips, which should that harvest reap,
At the wood's boldness by thee blushing stand!
To be so tickled they would change their state
And situation with those dancing chips,
O'er whom thy fingers walk with gentle gait,
Making dead wood more blessed than living lips.
    Since saucy jacks so happy are in this,
    Give them thy fingers, me thy lips to kiss.

ENVYING THOSE TICKLED IVORIES

WHEN I HEAR YOU, who are my music, play on the lucky keys whose motion sings at your sweet fingers, when you gently evoke from the strings a harmony that amazes my ears, I often envy those nimble keys that leap up to kiss the tender underside of your hand.

My luckless lips, which should be reaping that bounty, hover near you and blush at the boldness of the keyboard. To be tickled that way, my lips would gladly change their place and their fleshy nature with those dancing chips. How your fingers traverse them with ladylike pace, and make dead ivory seem more blessed than living lips!

Since those saucy keys are happy enough with this arrangement, give them your fingers to kiss, but me your lips.

Note: The mistress, presumably, is playing the virginals, a flat, legless harpsichord, probably so-called because typically played by young ladies presumed to be virgins. / L1: in S8 the Fair Youth is also called the poet's music. / L9: in S29 the poet scorned to change his state. / Ls 5 ,13: *jacks*: W.S. seems to have thought the fingers touched the jacks, but rather they strike the keys that strike the jacks that strike the wires.

129

*T*he expense of spirit in a waste of shame
    Is lust in action; and till action, lust
Is perjured, murderous, bloody, full of blame,
Savage, extreme, rude, cruel, not to trust,
Enjoyed no sooner but despised straight,
Past reason hunted, and no sooner had,
Past reason hated as a swallowed bait
On purpose laid to make the taker mad:
Mad in pursuit, and in possession so;
Had, having, and in quest to have, extreme,
A bliss in proof, and proved, a very woe;
Before, a joy proposed; behind, a dream.
    All this the world well knows, yet none knows well
    To shun the heaven that leads men to this hell.

LUST: BEFORE
AND AFTER

PURE LUST IN ACTION is a squandering of
vitality in a shameful waste. Before lust masters you,
you condemn it as deceitful, lethal, brutal, guilty,
animalistic, excessive, crude, cruel, and faithless.

Lust, moreover, is no sooner enjoyed than
despised. It is pursued beyond reason. Once indulged,
it is hated beyond reason. You detest lust as though
it were a bait deliberately laid to make the swallower
mad—mad in the hunting and mad in the having.

Whether you have indulged, are indulging, or are
trying to indulge, lust is too much. It is a bliss when
you are enjoying it, but a genuine grief afterwards.
It is a solid joy in anticipation, a dreamy wisp in
retrospect.

All this everybody understands very well. But
nobody knows how to shun the heaven that leads to
this hell.

Note: G.B. Shaw called this impersonal sonnet "the most merciless passage
in English literature." Another critic found it "the most completely powerful
sonnet in our literature." Later, in *King Lear* (4.6.126–7), W.S. warned: "But to
the girdle do the gods inherit; Beneath is all the fiends." In *Troilus and Cressida*
(3.1.81–3) he defines "the monstruosity [sic] in love...that the will is infinite and
the execution confined; that the desire is boundless and the act a slave to limit."

130

My mistress' eyes are nothing like the sun;
Coral is far more red than her lips' red;
If snow be white, why then her breasts are dun;
If hairs be wires, black wires grow on her head.
I have seen Roses damasked, red and white,
But no such Roses see I in her cheeks;
And in some perfumes is there more delight
Than in the breath that from my mistress reeks.
I love to hear her speak, yet well I know
That music hath a far more pleasing sound;
I grant I never saw a goddess go;
My mistress, when she walks, treads on the ground.
    And yet, by heaven, I think my love as rare
    As any she belied with false compare.

SHALL I COMPARE HER?

THE EYES OF my mistress are no sun in their shining. Coral is far more red than her lips. Compared with snow, her breasts are a dull gray. If hairs are golden strings, those on her head are black. I've seen damask Roses, red or white; I see no such Roses in her cheeks.

In many perfumes I take more delight than in the breath she exhales. I love to hear her speak, yet I am well aware that music has a sound far more agreeable. I admit that I've never seen a goddess in motion; but when my mistress walks, her feet touch the ground.

Yet, by heaven, I think my beloved is as rare as any woman all dolled up in the lies of extravagant comparisons.

Note: Almost line for line, the poet is here playing with a contemporary poem by Thomas Watson: *The Passionate Centurie of Love.* / It is striking that in these commonly called "Dark Lady" sonnets the mistress is only once called *dark* (S147) and never a lady. / It is fun to compare this sonnet with "Shall I compare you to a summer's day?" (S18). S141 is a kind of twin of this one.

131

*T*hou art as tyrannous, so as thou art,
   As those whose beauties proudly make them
      cruel;
For well thou know'st to my dear doting heart
Thou art the fairest and most precious jewel.
Yet in good faith some say that thee behold,
Thy face hath not the power to make love groan;
To say they err, I dare not be so bold,
Although I swear it to myself alone.
And to be sure that is not false I swear,
A thousand groans, but thinking on thy face,
One on another's neck, do witness bear
Thy black is fairest in my judgement's place.
   In nothing art thou black save in thy deeds,
   And thence this slander, as I think, proceeds.

CHARM VS. HARM

NOT EVEN YOUR FLAWS keep you from being as despotic as those women whose arrogant beauty makes them cruel. For you know very well that in my doting estimation you are a flawless and most precious jewel.

Still, some who have seen your face claim sincerely that it lacks the power to evoke the sighs of love. I am not bold enough to tell them they are wrong.

But in private I swear that they are. For thinking about your face, I groan a thousand groans. These prove that such swearing is not perjury. One after the other, they bear witness to my claim that your dark complexion is truly fair.

Only your deeds blacken you. And these, I believe, are the source of your demeaning reputation.

Note: Of these final 28 sonnets, only 17 directly address the mistress—and only as *thou*, never *you*, as the Fair Youth was sometimes addressed. (For the difference, see S13.) Seven sonnets talk about her; four have no explicit link with her.

132

*T*hine eyes I love, and they, as pitying me,
　　Knowing thy heart torments me with
　　　　disdain,
Have put on black, and loving mourners be,
Looking with pretty ruth upon my pain.
And truly not the morning sun of heaven
Better becomes the grey cheeks of the east,
Nor that full star that ushers in the even
Doth half that glory to the sober west
As those two mourning eyes become thy face.
O! let it then as well beseem thy heart
To mourn for me, since mourning doth thee grace,
And suit thy pity like in every part.
　　Then will I swear beauty herself is black,
　　And all they foul that thy complexion lack.

MOURNING BECOMES YOU

I LOVE YOUR EYES. They know that your heart torments me with contempt. So, commiserating with me, they dress in black and turn into tender mourners, looking on my pain with pretty pity.

Those two doleful eyes adorn your face more than heaven's morning sun beautifies the gray cheeks of the East. The luminous planet that ushers in the evening gives to the somber West not half the glory that your eyes give your face.

Since mourning becomes you, O let it then seem fitting for your heart as well to mourn me. Indeed, let that pity similarly invade your every part.

If these changes occur, I will swear that beauty herself is dark, and every woman ugly who lacks your complexion.

Note: L1: there is nothing about "poetry" or lamented "absences" in these 28 Dark Lady sonnets. But they are full of *eyes*, with 25 instances in 13 sonnets, plus five references of blindness. / L7: the evening star is usually Venus, though sometimes Mercury. / L9: we first met these mourning eyes in S127, which has a similar theme. *Mourning*, of course, plays with *morning*.

133

*B*eshrew that heart that makes my heart to
    groan

For that deep wound it gives my friend and me!

Is't not enough to torture me alone,

But slave to slavery my sweet'st friend must be?

Me from myself thy cruel eye hath taken,

And my next self thou harder hast engrossed:

Of him, myself, and thee, I am forsaken,

A torment thrice threefold thus to be crossed.

Prison my heart in thy steel bosom's ward,

But then my friend's heart let my poor heart bail;

Whoe'er keeps me, let my heart be his guard;

Thou canst not then use rigour in my jail.

   And yet thou wilt; for I, being pent in thee,

   Perforce am thine, and all that is in me.

MY SECOND SELF, YOUR SECOND PRISONER

THE DEVIL TAKE that heart of yours! For it makes my heart groan from the deep wounds which your heart inflicts on my friend and myself. Isn't it enough that your heart tortures me without enslaving my sweetest friend as well?

Your cruel eyes have already robbed me of myself. Now you have bound my second self to you even more tightly than you have bound me. And thus I lose him, myself, and you. To be so frustrated is thrice a triple torment.

Go ahead, lock up my heart in the steely cell of your breast—as long as you let my miserable heart encase the heart of my friend. No matter who my guard is, let my heart guard for my friend. Since he will then be safe within my custody, you won't be able to torment him.

But, alas, you will. For being locked inside you, I am necessarily yours, along with everything that is within me.

Note: Here a male friend enters the love scene to form a *ménage à trois*. The usual assumption is that this sweetest friend is the Fair Youth of the main set of sonnets. (See especially Ss 40 to 42.) Meanwhile, the pitying eye of the previous sonnet has now become cruel.

So now I have confessed that he is thine,
    And I myself am mortgaged to thy will,
Myself I'll forfeit, so that other mine
Thou wilt restore, to be my comfort still:
But thou wilt not, nor he will not be free,
For thou art covetous, and he is kind;
He learned but surety-like to write for me
Under that bond that him as fast doth bind.
The statute of thy beauty thou wilt take,
Thou usurer, that put'st forth all to use,
And sue a friend came debtor for my sake.
So him I lose through my unkind abuse.
    Him have I lost; thou hast both him and me;
    He pays the whole, and yet am I not free.

DOUBLE JEOPARDY

ALL RIGHT, MISTRESS MINE: I have admitted that my friend is your slave, and that I myself am mortgaged to your appetite. So I'll forfeit myself. Perhaps as a consolation prize you'll restore to me my friend and second self.

But you won't do it, nor will he choose to be liberated. For you are greedy and he is trying to be kind to me. On my behalf he signed his name on a bond of proxy that obligates him to you just as strongly as I was already bound.

To get your way with a friend of mine who became a debtor for my sake, you will invoke the law of your beauty. For you are a usurer, and turn everything into a loan. So I lose him, thanks to the harsh legalities in which I've entangled him.

Yes, I've lost him; and now you own both of us. He satisfies you completely, but you still won't give me my freedom.

Note: A number of surviving documents pertain to W.S. the businessman—a highly successful one. In this sonnet and others, technical words like *mortgaged*, *forfeit*, and *surety* bespeak a man acquainted with both legal and financial affairs. / Critic Stephen Booth nicely calls the next two sonnets "festivals of verbal ingenuity."

135

*W*hoever hath her wish, thou hast thy Will
And Will *to boot, and* Will *in overplus;*
More than enough am I that vex thee still,
To thy sweet will making addition thus.
Wilt thou, whose will is large and spacious,
Not once vouchsafe to hide my will in thine?
Shall will in others seem right gracious,
And in my will no fair acceptance shine?
The sea, all water, yet receives rain still,
And in abundance addeth to his store;
So thou, being rich in Will *add to thy* Will
One will of mine, to make thy large Will *more.*
    Let no unkind, no fair beseechers kill;
    Think all but one, and me in that one Will.

WHY REJECT ONLY ME?

OTHER WOMEN HAVE their wishes, but you have your *Will*, and *Will* in addition, and *Will* to excess. It is true that I who pester you all the time would be more than you needed if I added my love gift to your sweet supply.

Your will is large and roomy. Will you not even once agree to hide mine in yours? Must willingness seem quite desirable in others, while no gracious consent shines on what I will?

The sea is all water. Still it welcomes the rain, and adds to its store, already abundant. Though you are rich in the *Will* to be sexual, add to your *Will* fulness one willie of mine, *Will*-ingly enlarging what is already capacious.

Let no unkindness kill an honest request. Regard all lovers as but a single lover, and think of me as the sole resident of your *Will*-ing space.

Note: W.S. the punster here mocks the madness of lust: in 14 lines he plays on his name 13 times (plus one *wilt*). *Will* could mean sexual desire, sexual activity, or sexual parts. / Oddly, in the original, *Will* is capitalized and italicized only 7 of the 13 times. Was *Will* also the name of the mistress's husband, and even of the rival lover too (*William* Herbert)? An *overplus*, indeed! / Almost 25 percent of English boys of W.S.'s day were Williams (like the 1066 Conqueror).

If thy soul check thee that I come so near,
  Swear to thy blind soul that I was thy Will,
And will, thy soul knows, is admitted there;
Thus far for love my love-suit, sweet, fulfil.
Will *will fulfil the treasure of thy love,*
Ay, fill it full with wills, and my will one.
In things of great receipt with ease we prove
Among a number one is reckoned none:
Then in the number let me pass untold,
Though in thy stores' account I one must be;
For nothing hold me, so it please thee hold
That nothing me, a something sweet to thee:
  Make but my name thy love, and love that still,
  And then thou lovest me, for my name is Will.

HERE'S AN EXCUSE FOR YOUR CONSCIENCE

IF YOUR CONSCIENCE reproves you because I got as close as I did, swear to your blind soul that I was your *Will*. As your soul knows, erotic will has a pass to your site.

O my sweetheart, lovingly allow my love-suit to advance that far. *Will* will fulfill your love's longing for treasure. Indeed, my one willie will make your treasure box seem stuffed with them.

In a large warehouse crammed with many items, we easily count one the same as none. By such a reckoning, consider me unlisted among your conquests, though I was surely one of them.

Count me as a nothing, so long as you embrace my nothingness as something sweet to you.

Make but my name the object of your desire, and keep loving it. Then you'll be loving me, since my name is *Will*.

Note: Only 7 *will*s this time, 3 capitalized. For the various meanings of *will* in Will's day, see S135. / L8: counting is frequent in the *Sonnets*: *all* (87 times), *every* (31), *nothing* (19), *none* (13), *once* (10). We find *twice, twain, twofold, three, threefold, four, five, nine,* and *ten,* (but no "six," "seven," or "eight"). Higher numbers include *twenty, forty, sixty, hundred, thousand* (3), and *million* (2).

*T*hou blind fool, Love, what dost thou to mine
    eyes,

That they behold, and see not what they see?

They know what beauty is, see where it lies,

Yet what the best is take the worst to be.

If eyes, corrupt by over-partial looks,

Be anchored in the bay where all men ride,

Why of eyes' falsehood hast thou forged hooks,

Whereto the judgement of my heart is tied?

Why should my heart think that a several plot

Which my heart knows the wide world's common

    place?

Or mine eyes seeing this, say this is not,

To put fair truth upon so foul a face?

    In things right true my heart and eyes have erred,

    And to this false plague are they now transferred.

MY EYES HAVE HOODWINKED MY HEART

LOVE, WHO ARE already a blind fool, what have you done to my eyes? They look, but they don't see what they behold. They know what beauty is and where it dwells, yet they mistake the least of it for the most.

Corrupted by obsession, my eyes are anchored in that bay where all men ride. Nevertheless, blind Love, why have you made fishhooks out of the deceits of my eyes, and snagged as well the judgment of my heart?

Why should my heart think that my mistress is a private garden when it knows she is every man's playing field? Why do my eyes see this truth but deny it, putting the mask of lovely truth on so foul a face?

My heart and my eyes have failed me in serious matters of truthfulness, and have now succumbed to this plague of lies.

Note: Ls 6, 10: *the bay where all men ride...the wide world's common place*: the mistress is portrayed as totally promiscuous. / L12: *fair* and *foul* reappear from S127. / L14: literal plagues hounded W.S.'s life: around his birth, some 200 Stratford inhabitants died from pestis. The 1592 outbreak closed London theaters for nearly two years, while at least 10,000 perished in the city. Possibly killing his only son, plagues also struck in 1594, '96, 1606, '08, and '09.

138

When my love swears that she is made of
　　truth
I do believe her, though I know she lies,
That she might think me some untutored youth,
Unlearned in the world's false subtleties.
Thus vainly thinking that she thinks me young,
Although she knows my days are past the best,
Simply I credit her false-speaking tongue:
On both sides thus is simple truth suppressed.
But wherefore says she not she is unjust?
And wherefore say not I that I am old?
O love's best habit is in seeming trust,
And age in love loves not to have years told.
　　Therefore I lie with her, and she with me,
　　And in our faults by lies we flattered be.

LYING TOGETHER

I KNOW SHE IS LYING, but when my beloved
swears that she is honesty itself, I believe her.
That way she can think of me as some naive yokel,
ignorant of the world's subtle frauds.

My vanity supposes that she thinks me young—
though she knows I'm past my prime. So I give
simple credence to her lying lips. Thus is plain truth
suppressed on either side.

But why doesn't she admit that she is unfaithful?
And why don't I confess that I am old? Because
in her case love's best garment is the semblance of
trustworthiness; and in mine, an older lover does
not enjoy telling his age.

Therefore I lie with her, and she lies with me: and
through our sinful lies we stroke each other.

Note: The mistress is presented not only as thieving and promiscuous; she
is also deceitful (like the poet himself). This sonnet and S144 underwent an
unauthorized publication in 1599. In that edition, L11 read: "O, Love's best
habit's a soothing tounge [sic]"—presumably, a tongue that reassures by
pretending to be trusting.

O! call not me to justify the wrong
  That thy unkindness lays upon my heart;
Wound me not with thine eye but with thy tongue;
Use power with power, and slay me not by art.
Tell me thou lovest elsewhere; but in my sight,
Dear heart, forbear to glance thine eye aside;
What need'st thou wound with cunning when thy
  might
Is more than my o'erpressed defence can bide?
Let me excuse thee: ah! my love well knows
Her pretty looks have been mine enemies,
And therefore from my face she turns my foes,
That they elsewhere might dart their injuries.
  Yet do not so; but since I am near slain,
  Kill me outright with looks, and rid my pain.

HERE'S ANOTHER EXCUSE; PLEASE DON'T USE IT

PLEASE DON'T ASK ME to find excuses for the wrongs your cruelty has inflicted on my heart. If you must, wound me in private with your tongue, but not in public with your wandering eye. Slay me when we're alone by using your power powerfully. Don't do it delicately in front of others.

Admit to me that you have other lovers. But, sweetheart, when I am out with you, please restrain your sidelong glances. Why do you need to wound me slyly when your impact is already more than my overwhelmed defenses can sustain?

All right, I will fabricate an excuse for you! Ah! my beloved is well aware that her pretty looks have injured me. Therefore she turns away those hostile eyes from my face, and shoots their harmful darts elsewhere. But don't look elsewhere! I'm already half dead. Better to kill me outright with your looks, and free me from my pain.

Note: Scholars remain in the dark about the Dark Lady. Besides John Florio's wife (cf. S78), candidates include Mary Fitton, Emilia Lanier, and a "madam" named Lucy Morgan (alias Lucy Negro). But paintings of Fitton (William Herbert's mistress) show her to be fair and gray-eyed. Lanier was the mistress of Lord Chamberlain Hunsdon, patron of the Chamberlain's Men, one of the theatrical companies to which W.S. belonged.

SONNET 139

140

Be wise as thou art cruel; do not press
My tongue-tied patience with too much
disdain,
Lest sorrow lend me words, and words express
The manner of my pity-wanting pain.
If I might teach thee wit, better it were,
Though not to love, yet, love, to tell me so;
As testy sick men, when their deaths be near,
No news but health from their physicians know.
For if I should despair, I should grow mad,
And in my madness might speak ill of thee;
Now this ill-wresting world is grown so bad,
Mad slanderers by mad ears believed be.

That I may not be so, nor thou belied,
Bear thine eyes straight, though thy proud heart
go wide.

GET SMART! DON'T PUSH ME TOO FAR

BE AS SHREWD as you are cruel. Don't test my tongue-biting patience with too much contempt. Otherwise sorrow may supply me with words, and words will express how much I am suffering from the pain you refuse to pity.

Let me teach you shrewdness: it would be smarter, my beloved, if you said that you love me even though you don't. For I'm like an ill-tempered patient close to death. To him, the doctor speaks only encouraging words.

If I despair, I will grow mad, and in my madness I might speak ill of you. Now that this world, in its hunger for scandal, so wickedly distorts everything, even demented defamers are believed by demented ears.

To keep me from such madness and yourself from lying gossip, fix your eyes on me, though your haughty heart ranges widely.

Note: Seven years after S140 appeared, W.S. died. His doctor and executor was John Hall, wed to his daughter, Susanna. They were buried on either side of the Bard. Her epitaph calls her "witty beyond her sex." Hart's notes on his patients do not, alas, include W.S. (who at age 52 may have died from malaria or a stroke. But see Note for S141). Hall's diary for late April 1616 states simply: "My father-in-law died on Thursday." The larger world took scant notice.

141

In faith, I do not love thee with mine eyes,
 For they in thee a thousand errors note.
But 'tis my heart that loves what they despise,
Who in despite of view is pleased to dote.
Nor are mine ears with thy tongue's tune delighted,
Nor tender feeling to base touches prone,
Nor taste, nor smell, desire to be invited
To any sensual feast with thee alone.
But my five wits nor my five senses can
Dissuade one foolish heart from serving thee,
Who leaves unswayed the likeness of a man,
Thy proud heart's slave and vassal wretch to be.
  Only my plague thus far I count my gain,
  That she that makes me sin awards me pain.

YOU ARE A PLAGUE WITH ONE REDEEMING FEATURE

FRANKLY, MY DEAR, I do not love you with my eyes, for they detect in you a thousand flaws. It is my heart that loves what my eyes disdain, and delights in doting, despite your appearance.

Neither do my ears rejoice in the tone of your voice. My delicate sensitivities are not inclined to kinky intimacies. Neither my sense of taste nor of smell hankers to be invited to any sensual banquet where you are the only other guest.

Despite all this, neither my five wits nor five senses can dissuade a single foolish heart from being your servant, a heart undeterred that abandons the semblance of a free man to become the slave and vassal of your haughty heart.

Only to this extent do I find profit in my plague: the woman who causes my sins also provides the penance for them.

Note: L9: *five wits*, mental gifts (perhaps to balance the five senses). / L13: *plague*: in the year of W.S.'s birth, 15 percent of Stratford died from the plague. He was to die shortly after his daughter Judith's wedding. John Ward was the local pastor when Judith died in 1662. Was she the source of Ward's 1660s diary entry: "Shakspear, Drayton, and Ben Jonson, had a merry meeting, and it seems drank too hard, for Shakspear died of a feavour there contracted"? W.S., already ill, and upset with his new son-in-law, had revised his two-month-old will only one month earlier.

142

Love is my sin, and thy dear virtue hate,
Hate of my sin, grounded on sinful loving:
O! but with mine compare thou thine own state,
And thou shalt find it merits not reproving;
Or if it do, not from those lips of thine
That have profaned their scarlet ornaments
And sealed false bonds of love as oft as mine,
Robbed others' beds' revenues of their rents.
Be it lawful I love thee, as thou lov'st those
Whom thine eyes woo as mine importune thee:
Root pity in thy heart, that when it grows,
Thy pity may deserve to pitied be.

If thou dost seek to have what thou dost hide,
By self-example mayst thou be denied!

I'M A SINNER, BUT YOU'RE NO SAINT

LOVE IS MY SIN, but your precious virtue is hate—namely, the hatred you feel for the sin I commit by lustful loving. But, please, compare your own situation with mine. You'll find I merit no disapproval. Or if I do, not from your lips.

As often as mine, your lips have profaned their sacred scarlet, and stamped their seal on fraudulent bonds of love. Those lips have stolen from the beds of others their rightful rent.

Why then shouldn't it be lawful for me to love you as much as you fancy other men—men whom your eyes woo as insistently as mine woo you?

Therefore nurture pity in your heart, so that when it grows ripe, it may inspire a needed pity for you. If you try to win from others the pity you hide from me, may your own example prompt them to frustrate you.

Note: L6: the sacred scarlet of lips may be a reference to the robes of Roman cardinals (like Wolsey), who are vowed to chastity. This sonnet confuses: what sins has each committed; which one(s) does the mistress hate; and which one(s) does the poet want her to commit out of pity?

143

Lo, as a careful housewife runs to catch
    One of her feathered creatures broke away,
Sets down her babe and makes all swift dispatch
In pursuit of the thing she would have stay;
Whilst her neglected child holds her in chase,
Cries to catch her whose busy care is bent
To follow that which flies before her face,
Not prizing her poor infant's discontent;
So runn'st thou after that which flies from thee,
Whilst I thy babe chase thee afar behind;
But if thou catch thy hope, turn back to me,
And play the mother's part, kiss me, be kind:
    So will I pray that thou mayst have thy Will,
    If thou turn back, and my loud crying still.

BABY ME!

IMAGINE A DUTIFUL HOUSEWIFE trying to catch a flighty chicken. She puts her baby down and runs off quickly in pursuit of something she wants to keep. The neglected child chases after her, crying and reaching out to grab hold of her.

But to the poor infant's howling, the mother pays no attention. Her energy is focused on seizing the fleeing creature in front of her.

Well, you too are running after something that flies from you, and I'm your child, chasing you from a distance. All right, then; if you capture what you pursue, turn back to me. Play the mother: kiss me, pamper me.

In the hope that you will turn back and hush my howls, I will even pray that you get what you Will.

Note: Like a scurrying chicken, this sonnet runs on as one long sentence. / L9: who is the fowl running from the mistress? her angry husband? the poet's youthful friend, now disenchanted? / L13: for this final *Will* (desire), see S135. The last two lines reveal the most desperate self-humiliation.

144

*T*wo loves I have of comfort and despair,
 Which like two spirits do suggest me still:
The better angel is a man right fair,
The worser spirit a woman coloured ill.
To win me soon to hell my female evil
Tempteth my better angel from my side,
And would corrupt my saint to be a devil,
Wooing his purity with her foul pride.
And whether that my angel be turned fiend
Suspect I may, but not directly tell;
But being both from me, both to each friend,
I guess one angel in another's hell.
 Yet this shall I ne'er know, but live in doubt,
 Till my bad angel fire my good one out.

HELL IS OTHER LOVERS

I HAVE TWO PASSIONS: one brings me comfort, the other, despair. Like two spirits, they whisper to me all the time. The better angel is a man quite winsome; the worse spirit, a woman of bad complexion.

To get me sooner into her hellish clutches, my female evil tries to draw my better angel from my side. She wants to corrupt my saint into a devil, wooing his pure self with her foul arrogance.

I suspect, but cannot directly prove, that my angel has already become a demon. But since they are both now separated from me, and are both friends of each other, I can only conjecture that each is in the other's hell.

I won't know for sure, but must live in doubt until my bad angel's fire drives my good one away.

Note: L2: *still*: constantly. / L5: the poet would more willingly go to hell if his best friend were already there. / L14: the bad angel's repelling fire may result merely from her being more of a hellion than her partner. It may also include a burning venereal disease which she has and he doesn't want (or want again). Like S138, this sonnet (with some variation) had been published without permission ten years earlier. / In his *First Inaugural Address* Lincoln, who knew and loved his Shakespeare, invoked "the better angels of our nature."

145

*T*hose lips that Love's own hand did make,
　　Breathed forth the sound that said "I hate,"
To me that languished for her sake;
But when she saw my woeful state,
Straight in her heart did mercy come,
Chiding that tongue that ever sweet
Was used in giving gentle doom,
And taught it thus anew to greet:
"I hate," she altered with an end,
That followed it as gentle day
Doth follow night, who like a fiend
From heaven to hell is flown away.
　　"I hate" from hate away she threw,
　　And saved my life, saying "not you."

THIS ANNE HATH
A WAY

I LANGUISHED FOR love of her. But her lips, molded by Love itself, breathed forth the words, "I hate you."

Yet when she realized my wretchedness, mercy at once seized her heart and chided a tongue which was sweet even when it gently uttered words of doom.

Her mercy taught her to grant me a fresh response, and give "I hate you" a different ending, a conclusion that followed as gentle day follows night, that demon which flew from heaven to hell.

Saving my life, she took the hate away from "I hate you" by saying "I hate you... not."

Note: Understandably dubbed the slightest of the *Sonnets*, S145 is unique in having only eight syllables to the line, instead of the normal ten. Is it a keepsake of the poet's courting days? At age 18 he married his pregnant sweetheart, Anne, who was older than he by half. At 19 he became a father. At 20 he had his last offspring, boy and girl twins. / L13: *hate away* is surely a pun on Anne's family name, "Hathaway" (living with a *heath* not far *away*; or, living near a *heath*—an open, uncultivated patch of land). If she knew of these sonnets and took them literally, did she revert to her first response? / The word "hell" from S144 may explain this sonnet's odd placement.

146

Poor soul, the centre of my sinful earth,
*   [Feeding] these rebel pow'rs that thee array;*
Why dost thou pine within and suffer dearth,
Painting thy outward walls so costly gay?
Why so large cost, having so short a lease,
Dost thou upon thy fading mansion spend?
Shall worms, inheritors of this excess,
Eat up thy charge? is this thy body's end?
Then, soul, live thou upon thy servant's loss,
And let that pine to aggravate thy store;
Buy terms divine in selling hours of dross;
Within be fed, without be rich no more:
*   So shalt thou feed on Death, that feeds on men,*
*   And Death once dead, there's no more dying then.*

STARVE THE BODY, STARVING SOUL!

O PAUPER SOUL, core of my sinful clay, nourisher of those rebel powers that robe your exterior! Why do you languish within, and endure privations, while you paint your outer walls with such costly cheer? The body's lease is so brief! Why then do you spend so extravagantly on a crumbling mansion? Will gnawing worms be the solitary inheritors of all your investments? Will this be the final triumph of the body?

Lest this be so, soul of mine, enrich yourself at the body's expense. Let it pine away as you increase your wealth. Make a bargain with the divine by selling off those hours you normally waste. Nourish what is within; let what is without go without.

That way you will profit from the decay which feeds on every mortal. When you have killed off what death kills off, there will be no more dying.

Note: Most probably a printer's error, the beginning of L2 in the original repeated the end of L1: *my sinful earth.* One expert thinks the second line should start with "Feeding." / This sonnet is unique in featuring an explicit spiritual theme. / L11 recalls the medieval selling of indulgences. / L14 echoes biblical words; "Who will deliver me from the body of this death?" (*Romans* 7:24); and "Death will be swallowed up in victory" (*Isaiah* 25:8/*I Corinthians* 15:54).

147

My love is as a fever, longing still
For that which longer nurseth the disease;
Feeding on that which doth preserve the ill,
The uncertain sickly appetite to please.
My reason, the physician to my love,
Angry that his prescriptions are not kept,
Hath left me, and I desperate now approve
Desire is death, which physic did except.
Past cure I am, now reason is past care,
And frantic-mad with evermore unrest;
My thoughts and my discourse as madmen's are,
At random from the truth vainly expressed;
    For I have sworn thee fair, and thought thee bright,
    Who art as black as hell, as dark as night.

PAST CARING IS
PAST CURING

MY PASSION IS like a fever, forever longing for what nurtures and protracts my disease, feeding on what sustains my illness, on whatever pleases my sick, moody appetite.

Common sense, my love doctor, has abandoned me in anger because I have not taken its advice.

Desperate, I now realize that "desire is death," this desire to which my doctor took exception. But I am beyond cure, now that reason has stopped caring.

I grow frantic and insane and increasingly restless. My thoughts and words are those of a lunatic, far afield from the medical wisdom spoken to me so uselessly.

I have even sworn that you are lovely, and considered you luminous. But you are black as hell and dark as night.

Note: L9: the poet reverses the proverb, "Past cure, past care." / L14: only here is the Dark Lady *dark.* / With this sonnet in mind, critic Helen Vendler claims: "One of the great accomplishments of the Dark Lady Sequence is [W.S.'s] invention of the frantic discourse of unrest." / L8: *Desire is death*— a very Buddhist statement. This is the last of 15 appearances of *death.* As W.S. summarizingly says in *The Two Noble Kinsmen* (1.5.15): "This world's a city full of straying streets,/And death the market-place where each one meets."

O me! what eyes hath love put in my head,
Which have no correspondence with true sight;
Or, if they have, where is my judgement fled,
That censures falsely what they see aright?
If that be fair whereon my false eyes dote,
What means the world to say it is not so?
If it be not, then love doth well denote
Love's eye is not so true as all men's: no.
How can it? O! how can Love's eye be true,
That is so vexed with watching and with tears?
No marvel then, though I mistake my view;
The sun itself sees not till heaven clears.

   O cunning Love! with tears thou keep'st me blind,
   Lest eyes well-seeing thy foul faults should find.

LOVE IS CLEVERLY BLIND…AND BLINDING

GOOD GRIEF! What sort of eyes has Love lodged in my head? They can't even see what's in front of them. Or if they do, what has happened to my judgment, which condemns as false what my eyes perceive as true?

That vision on which my eyes dote, is it genuinely lovely? Then why does everybody say that it isn't? And if it isn't lovely, then being in love means that Love's eyes are not true, but everybody else's denial is.

But how can loving eyes see clearly when they are strained with watching and cloudy with tears? It's no wonder that I mistake what I see. Even the sun can't see the earth until the sky clears.

O tricky Love! You keep me blind from weeping. Otherwise, clear-sighted eyes would detect your ugly deficiencies.

Note: The blindness of the poet with respect to the Dark Lady is a repeated theme: see Ss 137, 138, 149, 150, and 152. In S141, though, his eyes could see all too clearly. W.S. had eye trouble too with the Fair Youth: see Ss 24, 46, 47, and 93. / Ls 13–14: some read this whole sonnet, or at least the final couplet, as addressed to the Dark Lady.

149

*C*anst thou, O cruel! say I love thee not,
   When I against myself with thee partake?
Do I not think on thee when I forgot
Am of myself, all tyrant, for thy sake?
Who hateth thee that I do call my friend?
On whom frown'st thou that I do fawn upon?
Nay, if thou lour'st on me, do I not spend
Revenge upon myself with present moan?
What merit do I in myself respect,
That is so proud thy service to despise,
When all my best doth worship thy defect,
Commanded by the motion of thine eyes?
   But, love, hate on, for now I know thy mind;
   Those that can see thou lovest, and I am blind.

WHY YOU HATE ME

YOU ARE HEARTLESS to say that I do not love you. How can you do so, when I take your side against my very self? Isn't it you whom I am remembering when, for your despotic sake, I have totally forgotten myself?

Have I befriended anyone who despises you? Or do I fawn on anyone who earns your scowl?

Indeed, if you scowl at me, do I not take revenge on myself through instant grief? Do I respect any gift of mine which haughtily refuses to be at your service? The fact is, that, commanded by a look from your eyes, all that is best in me worships your very flaws.

But hate on, my beloved, for now I know your preferences: you love those who can see truly, whereas I am uncritically blind.

Note: L14: We are nearing the end of *Shakespeare's Sonnets*. They record "joys, desires, revulsions, hurts, suspicions, jealousies, contentment, hopes, fears, depression, elation, tenderness, devotion, enthrallment by beauty, self-doubts, anger, recriminations, disgusts, conflict, reconciliations, courtings, yearning in absence, generosities, selfishness, dependence, dread of rejection, offenses, remorse, shame, obsession, dreams of the beloved, sleeplessness, aggression, idealizations, contempt, disappointments, confessions, and concealments." (Joseph Pequigney, *Such is My Love*.) Such is love, says the honest poet.

150

O! from what pow'r hast thou this pow'rful
                          might
With insufficiency my heart to sway,
To make me give the lie to my true sight,
And swear that brightness doth not grace the day?
Whence hast thou this becoming of things ill,
That in the very refuse of thy deeds
There is such strength and warrantise of skill
That, in my mind, thy worst all best exceeds?
Who taught thee how to make me love thee more,
The more I hear and see just cause of hate?
O, though I love what others do abhor,
With others thou shouldst not abhor my state:
    If thy unworthiness raised love in me,
    More worthy I to be beloved of thee.

YOUR VERY UNWORTHINESS TURNS ME ON

FROM WHAT SOURCE do you draw the mighty power to make your very deficiencies seduce my heart? to make me call my accurate vision deceptive? to swear against such certitudes as that brightness comes with daylight?

Where do you get the capacity to make evil things attractive? In the very trash of your doings such potency and surety of talent dwell that in my mind your worst totally surpasses everybody else's best.

Who taught you how to make me love you more, the more I hear and witness reasonable cause for detesting you? Though I love what others hate, you shouldn't join with them in loathing my situation. For if your very lack of deserving aroused love in me, I am the more deserving to be loved by you.

Note: L4: Since the Dark Lady is paradoxically a glittering lady of the night, the poet, to please her, swearingly denies the right of daytime to be called bright. / *Warning:* The Folger Library's commentary on *Shakespeare's Sonnets* apparently deemed the next sonnet so bawdy that it limited itself to one delicate sentence, and left most of the explanatory page blank.

151

Love is too young to know what conscience is,
*   Yet who knows not conscience is born of love?*
Then, gentle cheater, urge not my amiss,
Lest guilty of my faults thy sweet self prove.
For, thou betraying me, I do betray
My nobler part to my gross body's treason:
My soul doth tell my body that he may
Triumph in love; flesh stays no farther reason,
But, rising at thy name, doth point out thee
As his triumphant prize. Proud of this pride,
He is contented thy poor drudge to be,
To stand in thy affairs, fall by thy side.
*   No want of conscience hold it that I call*
*   Her "love" for whose dear love I rise and fall.*

NAIVE LOVE HAS
NO CONSCIENCE

LIKE THE CHILD CUPID, love is too immature to
know what conscience is. Yet everyone knows that
conscience is born of love. Then, my gentle cheat of a
mistress, do not incite me (again) to misbehavior, or
you will make your sweet self responsible for my sins.

For if you betray our virtuous resolution, I will
betray my nobler self into my gross body's treason.
My soul may then give my body permission to go
all the way in loving.

My carnal self will need no additional
permission. It will rise up at your name and point
you out as its triumphant prize. Proud of its victory,
my manhood will be happy to be your miserable
slave, to rise on your behalf, and fall at your side.

So do not think that I lack conscience when I
call her "love" for whose treasured affection I rise
and fall.

Note: L1: for W.S. *conscience* meant consciousness, moral judgment, and/or
sexual awareness. / L2: Does loving someone first make you aware of right
and wrong? / L3: *cheater*: promising all but not delivering? or cheating on
some virtuous resolve? / L13–14: when W.S. called his mistress "love," she
had apparently accused him of lacking conscience—though we're not told just
why (his marriage?). / As S142 perhaps does, S151 implies that W.S.'s passion
has not yet been fully consummated. But are the poems factual or
in chronological order?

152

In loving thee thou know'st I am forsworn,
    But thou art twice forsworn to me love
        swearing,
In act thy bed-vow broke, and new faith torn
In vowing new hate after new love bearing.
But why of two oaths' breach do I accuse thee,
When I break twenty? I am perjured most;
For all my vows are oaths but to misuse thee
And all my honest faith in thee is lost.
For I have sworn deep oaths of thy deep kindness,
Oaths of thy love, thy truth, thy constancy,
And, to enlighten thee, gave eyes to blindness,
Or made them swear against the thing they see:
    For I have sworn thee fair; more perjured eye,
    To swear against the truth so foul a lie!

BROKEN VOWS ON EVERY SIDE

YOU MUST REALIZE that by loving you I have become an oath-breaker. But you have broken two oaths: swearing love to me, you actively broke your marriage vow; now you have violated this new bond by vowing to reject me when you find a new lover.

But why do I accuse you of breaking two oaths when I have broken a score? I am the greater perjurer. For all my vows are sworn so that I can take advantage of you. All my honesty and faithfulness have been betrayed on your behalf.

For I have taken oaths by your deep kindness, by your love, by your truth, by your fidelity. To make you shine, I surrendered my eyes to blindness, and made them swear against what they actually saw.

Indeed, I have sworn that you are lovely. The more perjured am I, to have sworn so foul a lie against truth itself.

Note: In this final sonnet to his mistress, the poet returns to the themes of his first poem about her (S127)—fair and foul. But now these opposites are angrily used against her. Still, he accepts more blame than he did in S142. / L13: the first half of this line is an exact repeat of the first part of L13 in S147.

153

*C*upid laid by his brand and fell asleep:
    A maid of Dian's this advantage found,
And his love-kindling fire did quickly steep
In a cold valley-fountain of that ground;
Which borrowed from this holy fire of Love
A dateless lively heat, still to endure,
And grew a seething bath, which yet men prove
Against strange maladies a sovereign cure.
But at my mistress' eye Love's brand new-fired,
The boy for trial needs would touch my breast;
I, sick withal, the help of bath desired,
And thither hied, a sad distempered guest,
    But found no cure: the bath for my help lies
    Where Cupid got new fire, my mistress' eyes.

A TALE OF CUPID'S TORCH

THE LOVE-GOD CUPID once laid aside his torch and fell asleep. A maid of Diana, the chaste moon-goddess, took advantage of his repose, and quickly plunged his Love-kindling fire into a cold fountain in a nearby valley.

That fountain borrowed from this holy flame of Love a bubbling heat that permanently endures. It became a seething bath in which men find even now a sovereign cure for curious maladies.

The torch was later rekindled by my mistress's eyes. Needing to test it out, the Love-boy Cupid touched my breast. Sick from Love, and desiring help from that fountain, I hastened to it as a sad and ailing guest. I found no cure. For the only bath that would help me resides in those eyes where Cupid found a fresh kindling for his torch.

Note: L1: in addition to the bow and arrow, a torch was Cupid's (phallic) emblem. / These last two sonnets are unique for being mere variations of each other, and rare in their use of mythology. In each, the poet takes the waters, but for him the waters don't take. For the Romans, Cupid (from Latin *cupido*, "I desire") was the son of Venus, goddess of love (whence "venereal"). He was often depicted as a naked, winged, blindfolded infant. At other times he was a mischievous boy who randomly wounded gods and humans with arrows that made them fall madly in love. Erotic Eros was his Greek counterpart.

154

*T*he little Love-god lying once asleep
        Laid by his side his heart-inflaming brand,
Whilst many nymphs that vowed chaste life to keep
Came tripping by; but in her maiden hand
The fairest votary took up that fire
Which many legions of true hearts had warmed;
And so the general of hot desire
Was sleeping by a virgin hand disarmed.
This brand she quenched in a cool well by,
Which from Love's fire took heat perpetual,
Growing a bath and healthful remedy
For men diseased; but I, my mistress' thrall,
        Came there for cure, and this by that I prove,
        Love's fire heats water, water cools not love.

CUPID PREVISITED?

ONCE UPON A TIME, the little Love-god Cupid lay sleeping, with his heart-inflaming torch resting by his side. Many nymphs sworn to chastity then came dancing nimbly by.

The fairest of these devotees of the chaste moon-goddess, Diana, seized with her maiden hand that fire which had warmed many legions of true hearts. Thus, while sleeping, was the master of burning passion disarmed by a virgin hand.

The nymph then quenched this torch in the coolness of a nearby well. From Love's scorching blaze the well absorbed perpetual heat, and became a bath of healing for men diseased by Love.

Enslaved to my mistress, I went there for a cure. But this is what I discovered: Love's flame can boil water, but water can never chill the fire of Love.

Note: L13: did the poet contract a disease from the Dark Lady? / Some critics think that S154 was an unpolished version of S153 accidentally included. If so, it affords a unique glimpse of W.S. editing his own manuscript. / And so conclude *Shakespeare's Sonnets*: the last of their 17,543 words is *love*, which also adorns the last opening line, and opens the last closing line. With 162 occurrences, *Shakespeare's Sonnets* average more than one *love* per sonnet. The key word appears 2,200 times in the complete works of William Shakespeare.

Appendix

Was There Really a Shakespeare?

A Bible teacher of mine once argued that Noah's Flood had to be local, since a global flood would have required "too great" a miracle.

Most admirers would agree that for anyone to have been Shakespeare was a miracle; but for lowly Shakespeare to have been Shakespeare—well, that's asking too much from the wonder department.

Still, there is absolutely no historical doubt that there was a William Shakespeare who was born in 1564 in Stratford-upon-Avon, England, had a wife and three children there, worked several decades in London as a theatre man, and retired again to Stratford until his death in 1616. He is buried there in the parish church, which possesses the records of his baptism and burial.

The only question (in some people's minds) is whether this is the man who wrote the glorious plays. For the first two centuries after his death, however, this question seems never to have found a serious mind ready to raise it. (The doubters are called anti-Stratfordians.)

This is not the place to list the main reasons for whatever doubt persists, nor to name the suggested authors who might have been hiding behind an actor's name at a time when plays were considered "trifles" rather than literature, and theatres were regarded as "Satan's Chapels."

I merely note that I share the wonder but not the doubt. The Master of Western and perhaps World Literature left no diaries, and no personal papers except his will. No letters from him have ever been found. So it is because the poet was such a colossal genius, and because so little is known about his inner life, that such interest is taken in the chance that his *Sonnets* might be autobiographical.

How Do You Spell That?

The original Shakespeare was presumably a fighter who at least knew how to shake a spear. The only English pope, Adrian IV (c.1100–1159), had the similar but even more valiant name of Breakspear.

The hyphenated Shake-Speare, which appears on the cover of the original *Sonnets,* may be puzzling. True, in the Bard's day, consistency in spelling was no virtue, and a choice might depend on local variations in pronunciation, or on the space available to a writer or typesetter. (Cf. George Wise's 1869 opus, *The Autograph of William Shakespeare…* Together with *4,000 Ways of Spelling the Name.*)

The earliest Shakespeare on record was also a William whose surname and life span were both briefer than usual. (For William, see S57.) This Saksper was hanged for theft in 1248. Seventeen spellings have been found for the poet's father's last name, though Shakspere is the most frequent. Perhaps in his environs the first syllable sounded like "shack," while in London, "shake" prevailed.

In literary documents Shakespeare is the spelling in about 90 percent of cases. And that's the way the poet himself signed the dedication of his first two long poems. However, the second most common spelling, Shake-Speare, appears on the title page of the plays *Richard II*, *Richard III*, and *Hamlet*.

In his six known autographs, the spelling Shakespeare is not used, nor did he spell his name the same way twice. He even wrote it two ways in his last will. These samples, however, are from the final years of his life, when he may have been suffering from writer's palsy and, at the end, from a stroke. There is no name on his replaced gravestone, with its famous "Good Frend for Jesus Sake Forbeare." Family members buried nearby, however, are identified in the modern spelling.

More Sonnet Context

Frederick the Second (1194–1250), the Wonder of his World (*Stupor Mundi*), and the grandson of Frederick Barbarossa, was raised in Sicily, which his Normandy ancestors had conquered from Islamic Arabs around the celebrated year 1066. Italian poetry was born in his encouraging shadow.

A linguist, poet, and pre-Renaissance Renaissance man, he created on the island, around Palermo, a scintillating literary court of Provençal troubadours, German minne-singers and others. On the adjacent mainland part of his kingdom, he founded the University of Naples (where his cousin Thomas Aquinas studied).

One of Frederick's secretary/lawyers was the Sicilian, Giacomo da Lentino. In Dante's *Purgatorio*, he is referred to merely as "the Notary"—as if everybody knew who he was. This Lentino is credited with creating the sonnet form. In the third decade of the 1200s, the "Sicilian School" of poets, preeminently Lentino, produced the earliest surviving sonnets, some 58 in all, nearly half by "the Notary."

In the introduction, the journey of the Sicilian sonnet was traced through northern Italy, France, and England. In 1598, a Cambridge cleric named Francis Meres published a book about the literary scene in England. He claimed that the sweet, witty soul of the ancient Roman poet Ovid (43 B.C.–17 A.D.) was now dwelling in the mellifluous and honey-tongued soul of a man named Shakespeare, as witness "his sugred Sonnets [circulating] among his private friends."

The very next year (1599), a William Jaggard published a small volume entitled *The Passionate Pilgrime*, by W. Shakespeare. Of the 20 sonnets in the book, only four were arguably Shakespeare's. The rest were no credit to his reputation.

So it is not surprising that the Bard was reported to have been "much offended" that Jaggard had "presumed to make so bold with his name." (Yet he was chosen to be the 1623 printer of the *First Folio* of Shakespeare's plays! In those days the best publishers were not especially interested in plays.)

The last six sonnets in Jaggard's book are prefaced with the words, "Sonnets to Sundry Notes of Musicke." Today we usually think of sonnets as something read or recited, not something sung. Yet its very name denotes that it is something to be "sounded," a songette. Because the traditional sonnet had a brief, fixed structure, regular rhythm, prominent, repetitive rhymes, and amorous themes, it would have been exceptionally apt for being put to music—unless, of course, the musical form came first. After all, a lyrical poem is one that is fit to be accompanied by the harp-like lyre.

As noted, the sonnet—and Italian poetry in general—was born among the court poets living in southern Italy/Sicily in the early 1200s. Before long the sonnet spread northward to Tuscany. Eighty-one sonnets are attributed to Dante the Tuscan (1265–1321).

But it was later in the century of Dante's death that the Florentine cleric Petrarch (1304–1374) brought the Italian sonnet to its pitch of perfection in his 317 published sonnets to and about the disdainful Laura, who (if she truly lived) died from the Black Death.

In the early 1500s the Italian sonnet was introduced into England and into English. Two young friends and translators, Sir Thomas Wyatt (1503–1542) and the

Earl of Surrey (Henry Howard, c. 1517–1547) are given credit for this historical development.

Wyatt seems to have written the first original English sonnets, while Surrey soon introduced into the sonnet form the wrap-up rhyming couplet, which Shakespeare favored. In addition, Surrey also pioneered English "blank [unrhymed] verse" in his translation of the poet Virgil.

Both friends spent time in prison on political charges. Surrey was a cousin of Henry VIII, whose paranoia led to Surrey's decapitation a few days before Henry's own death. A decade later the sonnets of both friends were included in the 1557 *Songs and Sonnets* (alias *Tottel's Miscellany*), the premier printed collection of English verse.

A few decades afterwards, Sir Philip Sidney (1554–1586) wrote the first influential sonnet sequence in the English language. (His sister Mary was the mother of William Herbert, a chief candidate for being the "W.H." of the *Sonnets*.)

Sidney's sequence, *Astrophel and Stella*, was published in 1591, after he had died a battle hero. The sequence is credited with sparking a decade of vigorous sonnet-writing in England. Scarcely in his thirties, Shakespeare was still new to London in the early 1590s, and he joined in the fad.

He even incorporates seven sonnets in his play of that period, *Love's Labour's Lost*. Composed later, the enchanting opening conversation between Romeo and Juliet is actually a sonnet [I, v, 93–106]: *If I profane with my unworthiest hand/This holy shrine, the gentle sin is this...*). At times, however, the playwright seems to be mocking sonnets, sonneteers, and their sonnetizing.

Early in the next century, John Donne (1572–1631) expanded the sonnet from almost exclusively romantic themes into religious ones ("Batter my heart, three-personed God").

Later that century John Milton of *Paradise Lost* (1608–1674) produced sonnets on political and even personal subjects (e.g., his blindness: "When I consider how my light is spent...").

[When Milton was 24, his first published poem appeared as an anonymous eulogy on Shakespeare in the *Second Folio* (1632). By a spectacular coincidence, Milton was born in a room near London's Mermaid Tavern, which the Bard and other literary stars frequented. One can imagine Shakespeare being interrupted in the reading of a new sonnet by the hearty squall of a new-born child nearby. His own book of *Sonnets* would come to birth within a year.]

In the 1800s English poets like Wordsworth ("The world is too much with us, late and soon..."), Keats ("Much have I travell'd in the realms of gold...") and Elizabeth Barrett Browning ("How do I love thee? Let me count the ways..."), reelectrified the sonnet tradition. The celebrated words, "Give me your tired, your poor..." are from an 1883 sonnet, *The New Colossus*, by New Yorker Emma Lazarus. Later the German poet Rainer Maria Rilke won international fame for his 1923 *Sonnets to Orpheus*.

Sonnet

All we need is fourteen lines, well, thirteen now,
and after this one just a dozen
to launch a little ship on love's storm-tossed seas,
then only ten more left like rows of beans.
How easily it goes unless you get Elizabethan
and insist the iambic bongos must be played
and rhymes positioned at the ends of lines,
one for every station of the cross.
But hang on here while we make the turn
into the final six where all will be resolved,
where longing and heartache will find an end,
where Laura will tell Petrarch to put down his pen,
take off those crazy medieval tights,
blow out the lights, and come at last to bed.

—BILLY COLLINS

The resilient sonnet form has proven itself unique in Western literature. For over five centuries major poets have continued to be attracted to this one particular verse form. Above is a sonnet about sonnets by Billy Collins, the former Poet Laureate Consultant to the Library of Congress. Though irregular in form, it takes us right back to Petrarch and his lady love, Laura.

TECHNICALITIES

What exactly is a sonnet? In its classical version, a sonnet is a poem of fourteen lines. The number fourteen is quite arbitrary, though it nicely allows for an internal mini-drama.

The influential Petrarch usually divided his fourteen lines into an octave (the first eight), and a sestet (the last six). Typically, the octave presents a theme, and the sestet develops it.

The rhymes of Petrarch's octave used the pattern of abba/abba. His sestet rhyme pattern varied, but never ended in the rhymed couplet that Shakespeare made so famous. The Petrarchan (or Italian) sonnet usually rhymes thus: the octave: abba/abba; the sestet: cde/cde or cd/cd/cd.

In English, the sonnet adopted the basic English prose beat: iambic (daDUM), repeated four times (pentameter). Thus: Shall I compare thee to a summer's day? The so-called Shakespearean sonnet often has three sets of four lines (three quatrains=twelve lines), followed by a rhymed couplet (two lines) for the traditional total of fourteen.

The usual English rhyme pattern is abab/cdcd/efef/gg. Thus the sonnet just cited ends with these sounds: day, ate, May, date/shines, dimmed, clines, trimmed/fade, ow'st, shade, grow'st/see, thee.

This rhyme scheme is variously called the Shakespearean Sonnet, the Elizabethan Sonnet (for Queen Elizabeth I), or the English Sonnet.

SHAKESPEARE'S SONNETS: CURIOSITIES

S5 and 23 others (about 15 percent) are addressed to no one in particular. S5 and 12 others have no first-person speaker. S5 and 4 others have neither first-person speaker nor addressee.

S25: in the original printing, L9 ends with "worth," which, uniquely, does not rhyme with its partner in L11. Editors sometimes replace "worth" with "fight" or "might." No one seems inclined to replace "quite" with a word rhyming with "worth."

S36 and S96 end with the same couplet.

S99 has 15 lines instead of 14.

S126 is not a sonnet but a set of six rhymed couplets, followed by two mysterious blank parentheses.

S138 and S144 had already been published in an unauthorized and slightly variant version in 1599 A.D., a decade earlier.

S145 has only 8 syllables to a line instead of 10.

S153 and S154 are variations of identical material.

WORDS, WORDS, WORDS

Especially in the modern computer age, you'd think it would be fairly easy to determine how many words Shakespeare wrote. But would that number include titles, stage directions, the names of speaking actors, and similar marginal matters?

And, most complicating of all, which plays/poems would you consider genuine, and which versions of those works? So it shouldn't be surprising that estimates range from 885,000 to 895,000 words. The *King James Bible* (published two years after the *Sonnets*, and including all disputed texts) has fewer words than that number.

Discovering how many different words Shakespeare used is even more problematic. For instance, consider *love*, a word which Shakespeare uses 2,200 times (162 times in 154 sonnets). In terms of basic vocabulary, are *lover*, *loves*, *loved*, *loving*, and *lovingly* independent words, or are they all *love* words?

Or take the word *pen*: is it one word, or does it become three words by the difference between 1) a writing instrument, and 2) a place for keeping pigs, babies, and prisoners, and 3) the internal horny shell of a squid.

These and other questions readily explain why you find even more wildly different answers to a second seemingly simple question: how big was Shakespeare's working vocabulary?

Again, estimates range from 15,000 to 32,000 words. A website check of various counts yields: more than 15,000, upward of 17,000, 21,000, 25,000, 29,066, some 30,000, and 31,534. The vocabulary of the *King James Bible* is a scant 8,000 words.

In any case, most scholars would agree that at a time when there were in effect no English dictionaries and no public libraries, the country boy from Stratford (pop: under 2,000) commanded the largest vocabulary in any language ever possessed by a writing member of the human race. Remarkably, more than 7,000 Shakespearean words are "nonce" words, i.e., used only once by Shakespeare.

But that's not the whole story. The authoritative *Oxford English Dictionary* cites nearly 3,000 words whose oldest written use is found in Shakespeare—for example, *assassination*, (a nonce word used in *Macbeth*, Abraham Lincoln's favorite play). These words comprise about 17 percent of his total vocabulary.

Though many new words must have already been in the air, the Bard himself undoubtedly coined many of the 17 percent. One source credits him with inventing over 1,700 common words.

And then there are household phrases first found in Shakespeare: e.g., *household words*, *brave new world*, *sea change*, *laughing-stock*, *dead as a doornail*, *an eye-sore*, *the apple of her eye*, *pomp and circumstance*, *into thin air*, *budge an inch*, *not a mouse stirring*, *the naked truth*, *to the manner born*, *good riddance*, *for goodness' sake*, and *knock, knock; Who's there?*

Appearing in *Love's Labour's Lost* (V, i, 41), is his longest word, obviously mock-scholarly: *honorificabilitudinitatibus*.

SONNET WORDS

The sonnet section of the 1609 book contains some 17,543 words. Its 2,156 lines make it longer than *Macbeth* or *The Comedy of Errors*.

Including the original 154 sonnets, this volume you are holding contains 58,956 words. That means that, on the average, this book devotes somewhat more than two words to each sonnet word.

Of the 17,543 sonnet words (which fit into 21,560 syllables), a remarkable 82 percent are monosyllables—those ancient, sturdy, racy words, good for packing a tight space and hammering home a point.

The *Sonnets* contain 3,274 different words, of which 2,015 words (62 percent) are "nonce" words with a single appearance within the *Sonnets*. The remaining 1,259 words are used multiple times—from twice, to as many as *love*'s 162 times.

Longest, Shortest Plays and All the Poems

Hamlet ....3,929 lines...29,551 words (1602)
The Comedy of Error...1,911 lines...14,369 words (1606)
The Sonnets...........2,156 lines...17,543 words (1609)
The Rape of Lucrece....1,855 lines...14,519 words (1594)
Venus and Adonis......1,194 lines.... 9,867 words (1593)
A Lover's Complaint.....329 lines.... 2,561 words (1609)
The Phoenix and
  the Turtle ....100 lines ......360 words (1600)

$\mathscr{R}$esources

Books

The Art of Shakespeare's Sonnets: Helen Vendler/ 1999

A Companion to Shakespeare's Sonnets: Michael Schoenfeldt/ 2010

The Oxford Shakespeare: The Complete Sonnets and Poems: Colin Burrow/ 2008

Sexual Shakespeare: Michael Keevak/ 2001

Shakespeare's Sonnets: Stephen Booth/ 2000

Shakespeare's Sonnets: Flo Gibson (Narrator) Audio Book Contractors

Shakespeare's Sonnets: Katherine Duncan-Jones/ 1997

Shakespeare's Sonnets & Poems (Folger Shakespeare Library): Paul Werstine and Dr. Barbara A. Mowat/ 2006

The Sonnets and a Lover's Complaint: John Kerrigan/ 2010

The Sonnets and Narrative Poems by William Shakespeare: Kindle Edition/ 2011

The Sonnets: The New Cambridge Shakespeare: G. Blakemore Evans and Stephen Orgel/ 2006

The Sonnets: A New Variorum Edition of Shakespeare/ Classic Publishers/ 1999

Such is My Love: Joseph Pequigney/ 1985

Note: Amazon.com lists 2,529 items under the heading "Shakespeare's Sonnets."

Websites

www.shakespearessonnets.com/index.html
detailed study of each sonnet;
www.shu.ac.uk/emls/Sonnets/Sonnets.html
facsimile of original sonnets;
www.concordance.com/cgi-bin/begnr.pl
a concordance of most sonnet words;
www.britannica.com/shakespeare/related links.html
W.S. life and related links;
shakespeare.palomar.edu
W.S. and the Internet

First Line Index

A woman's face with Nature's own hand painted	62
Accuse me thus: that I have scanted all	256
Against my love shall be, as I am now	148
Against that time, if ever that time come	120
Ah! wherefore with infection should he live	156
Alack! what poverty my Muse brings forth	228
Alas! 'tis true, I have gone here and there	242
As a decrepit father takes delight	96
As an unperfect actor on the stage	68
As fast as thou shalt wane, so fast thou grow'st	44
Be wise as thou art cruel; do not press	302
Being your slave, what should I do but tend	136
Beshrew that heart that makes my heart to groan	288
Betwixt mine eye and heart a league is took	116
But be contented when that fell arrest	170
But do thy worst to steal thyself away	206
But wherefore do not you a mightier way	54
Canst thou, O cruel! say I love thee not	320
Cupid laid by his brand and fell asleep	328
Devouring Time, blunt thou the lion's paws	60
Farewell! thou art too dear for my possessing	196
For shame deny that thou bear'st love to any	42
From fairest creatures we desire increase	24

From you have I been absent in the spring	218
Full many a glorious morning have I seen	88
How can I then return in happy plight	78
How can my Muse want subject to invent	98
How careful was I, when I took my way	118
How heavy do I journey on the way	122
How like a winter hath my absence been	216
How oft, when thou, my music, music play'st	278
How sweet and lovely dost thou make the shame	212
I grant thou wert not married to my Muse	186
I never saw that you did painting need	188
If my dear love were but the child of state	270
If the dull substance of my flesh were thought	110
If there be nothing new, but that which is	140
If thou survive my well-contented day	86
If thy soul check thee that I come so near	294
In faith, I do not love thee with mine eyes	304
In loving thee thou know'st I am forsworn	326
In the old age black was not counted fair	276
Is it for fear to wet a widow's eye	40
Is it thy will thy image should keep open	144
Let me confess that we two must be twain	94
Let me not to the marriage of true minds	254
Let not my love be called idolatry	232
Let those who are in favour with their stars	72
Like as the waves make towards the pebbled shore	142
Like as, to make our appetites more keen	258

FIRST LINE INDEX

Lo, as a careful housewife runs to catch	308
Lo! in the orient when the gracious light	36
Look in thy glass, and tell the face thou viewest	28
Lord of my love, to whom in vassalage	74
Love is my sin, and thy dear virtue hate	306
Love is too young to know what conscience is	324
Mine eye and heart are at a mortal war	114
Mine eye hath played the painter and hath steeled	70
Music to hear, why hear'st thou music sadly?	38
My glass shall not persuade me I am old	66
My love is as a fever, longing still	316
My love is strengthened, though more weak in seeming	226
My mistress' eyes are nothing like the sun	282
My tongue-tied Muse in manners holds her still	192
No longer mourn for me when I am dead	164
No more be grieved at that which thou hast done	92
No, Time, thou shalt not boast that I do change	268
Not from the stars do I my judgement pluck	50
Not marble nor the gilded monuments	132
Not mine own fears, nor the prophetic soul	236
O how thy worth with manners may I sing	100
O me! what eyes hath love put in my head	318
O that you were yourself! but, love, you are	48
O thou my lovely boy, who in thy power	274
O truant Muse, what shall be thy amends	224
O, how much more doth beauty beauteous seem	130
O! call not me to justify the wrong	300

O! for my sake do you with Fortune chide	244
O! from what pow'r hast thou this pow'rful might	322
O! how I faint when I of you do write	182
O! lest the world should task you to recite	166
O! never say that I was false of heart	240
Or I shall live your epitaph to make	184
Or whether doth my mind, being crowned with you	250
Poor soul, the centre of my sinful earth	314
Say that thou didst forsake me for some fault	200
Shall I compare thee to a summer's day?	58
Sin of self-love possesseth all mine eye	146
Since brass, nor stone, nor earth, nor boundless sea	152
Since I left you, mine eye is in my mind	248
So am I as the rich whose blessed key	126
So are you to my thoughts as food to life	172
So is it not with me as with that Muse	64
So now I have confessed that he is thine	290
So oft have I invoked thee for my Muse	178
So shall I live, supposing thou art true	208
Some glory in their birth, some in their skill	204
Some say thy fault is youth, some wantonness	214
Sweet love, renew thy force; be it not said	134
Take all my loves, my love, yea, take them all	102
That god forbid that made me first your slave	138
That thou art blam'd shall not be thy defect	162
That thou hast her, it is not all my grief	106
That time of year thou mayst in me behold	168

That you were once unkind befriends me now	262
The expense of spirit in a waste of shame	280
The forward violet thus did I chide	220
The little Love-god lying once asleep	330
The other two [elements], slight air and purging fire	112
Then hate me when thou wilt; if ever, now	202
Then let not winter's ragged hand deface	34
They that have power to hurt and will do none	210
Thine eyes I love, and they, as pitying me	286
Those hours, that with gentle work did frame	32
Those lines that I before have writ do lie	252
Those lips that Love's own hand did make	312
Those parts of thee that the world's eye doth view	160
Those pretty wrongs that liberty commits	104
Thou art as tyrannous, so as thou art	284
Thou blind fool, Love, what dost thou to mine eyes	296
Thus can my love excuse the slow offence	124
Thus is his cheek the map of days outworn	158
Thy bosom is endeared with all hearts	84
Thy gift, thy tables, are within my brain	266
Thy glass will show thee how thy beauties wear	176
'Tis better to be vile than vile esteemed	264
Tired with all these, for restful death I cry	154
To me, fair friend, you never can be old	230
Two loves I have of comfort and despair	310
Unthrifty loveliness, why dost thou spend	30
Was it the proud full sail of his great verse	194

Weary with toil, I haste me to my bed	76
Were't aught to me I bore the canopy	272
What is your substance, whereof are you made	128
What potions have I drunk of Siren tears	260
What's in the brain that ink may character	238
When forty winters shall besiege thy brow	26
When I consider every thing that grows	52
When I do count the clock that tells the time	46
When I have seen by Time's fell hand defac'd	150
When in the chronicle of wasted time	234
When most I wink, then do mine eyes best see	108
When my love swears that she is made of truth	298
When thou shalt be disposed to set me light	198
When to the sessions of sweet silent thought	82
When, in disgrace with Fortune and men's eyes	80
Where art thou, Muse, that thou forget'st so long	222
Whilst I alone did call upon thy aid	180
Who is it that says most, which can say more	190
Who will believe my verse in time to come	56
Whoever hath her wish, thou hast thy Will	292
Why didst thou promise such a beauteous day	90
Why is my verse so barren of new pride	174
Your love and pity doth th'impression fill	246

About the Author

Joseph Gallagher was born in Baltimore on June 19, 1929, and ordained a priest for the Baltimore Archdiocese on May 28, 1955.

He served as an editor of the *Baltimore Catholic Review* from 1959 to 1966, and was Archdiocesan Archivist from 1957 to 1966.

He taught at Baltimore's St. Mary's Seminary, and lectured locally at Johns Hopkins University, Notre Dame College, and Loyola College. He taught at Oxford, England for Antioch International in 1977. His chief subjects were public speaking, philosophy, poetry, and other literary topics such as *The Divine Comedy* and Shakespeare's *Sonnets*.

He was translator and translation editor for *The Documents of Vatican II* (1966), and executive editor for the bicentennial edition of *The American Catholic's Who's Who*.

He has published three books of poems, *Painting on Silence* (1973), *Statements at the Scene* (1998), and an *80th Birthday Collection* (2009).

Other publications are a book of memoirs, *The Pain and the Privilege: The Diary of a City Priest* (Doubleday, 1983) and *The Christian Under Pressure* (1970). The latter was reprinted in 1988 as *How to Survive Being Human*, and again in 2010 under the same title.

In 1987 Sheed and Ward published his booklet, *Voices of Strength and Hope for a Friend with AIDS*.

He has published in half a hundred publications, including *The National Catholic Reporter*, *America*, and *The New York Times*.

He received a Master's degree in 1972 from the Johns Hopkins University's Creative Writing Seminars.

His latest book, *Watch Your Language*, was published by Amazon/Createspace in late 2010.